Things That Go Bump in the Night

By the same author:

Discover Tarot
Tarot Prediction

Things That Go Bump in the Night

How to Investigate and Challenge Ghostly Experiences

Emily Peach

The Aquarian Press
An Imprint of HarperCollins*Publishers*

The Aquarian Press
An Imprint of Grafton Books
A Division of HarperCollins*Publishers*
77–85 Fulham Palace Road,
Hammersmith, London W6 8JB

Published by The Aquarian Press 1991

1 3 5 7 9 10 8 6 4 2

British Library Cataloguing in Publication Data
Peach, Emily
Things that go bump in the night: how to
challenge and interpret ghostly experiences
1. Ghosts
I. Title
133.1

0-85030-873-9

Printed in Great Britain by
Mackays of Chatham, Kent

For Geoffrey

From ghoulies and ghosties and long-leggety beasties
And things that go bump in the night,
Good Lord, deliver us!

Contents

— *Part 1* —

FACTS

— *1* —

Preconceptions

The evidence for the existence of ghosts is vast and incontrovertible. Thousands upon thousands of recorded experiences, taken from sources all over the world and ranging over many centuries, all agree as to their existence, their nature and their behaviour. To seriously question their empirical reality, one would have to postulate an enormous and on-going conspiracy spanning countless centuries and involving such diverse individuals as Plato, Pliny, Cicero and Mrs S. from Croydon. Statistics suggest that as many as one person in ten may have dealings with a ghost of some kind during the course of his adult life. Yet still nobody believes in ghosts, and everybody persists in asking the same questions about them whenever the subject comes up.

Why do we go on quarrelling about the existence of something we ourselves have proved to exist many times? Why do people keep saying that ghosts don't exist, that only gullible people believe in them and only mad people see them — and whence the (questionable) evidence to back these claims up? And why, when we question the reality or otherwise of these elusive and controversial creatures, must most of our questions be directed (as it seems they must), not at the evidence for the existence of ghosts, but, with subtle and insidious bias, at the mental condition of the people who see them? A few sandwiches short of a picnic. Only 80 pence in the pound. A bit tapped. Is it really possible that perhaps one person in ten actually conforms to these peculiar criteria?

Of course it is not. But the paranormal is a subject which, albeit perennially interesting, is also extremely dangerous in its implications. It is certainly odd that the human race should be so willing to seriously question the sanity of some thousands of its members, but it is in no way incomprehensible.

Ghosts do not fit into the iron straitjacket of human preconceptions about life, the universe and everything, and cannot be made to do so, but humanity as a whole has a vested interest in preserving those preconceptions intact. Man has frequently been taught — and has always liked to believe — that he understands his world and everything in it, and also that he can with impunity alter and control it. The bizarre, the paranormal, the odd and the apparently inexplicable can have no place within the parameters of such a narrow philosophy. Were they to be given houseroom in the corporate reality spectrum they would of necessity knock holes in all man's most cherished beliefs, rock his commonplace and extremely comfortable view of his world and shake the rules of his existence to their very foundations. Psychically, those treasured preconceptions stand between man and an unpredictable and potentially dangerous universe. The level of fear he experiences when they are shown to be groundless or misplaced is therefore very acute, and he will go to any lengths, sacrifice any number of his fellow men, and render himself to all intents and purposes both blind and deaf to avoid such a threat. Effectively, humanity as a body refuses to believe in ghosts because it cannot afford to do otherwise, and thus its questions and answers about ghosts (and a good many other things, for that matter) are uniformly facile, childish and simply self-revealing. Furthermore, humanity's prejudices against ghosts must extend to embrace those few of its number who will not, or perforce cannot, share those prejudices. Those who by their very existence lever open the shutters so carefully closed in the corporate mind and force everyone to look out into the twilight zone of the unknown and confront the monsters standing there must be defined as 'traitors' and made pariahs by the majority if the precarious status is to remain anywhere near quo. Ordinary people with extraordinary beliefs or extraordinary experiences to relate are not popular and, indeed, are fated to be mocked and ridiculed into seemly silence. Should they refuse to be silenced, then they are labelled 'mad' — which achieves much the same result in the end. As a solution to life's mysteries this behaviour is, of course, neither satisfactory nor very scientific, but it is certainly effective.

Because of the very general unwillingness to look the scientific facts of life about ghosts firmly in the face, the man in the street's preconceptions about them — their nature, their behaviour, and the rules that govern them — are culled primarily from fiction, and those preconceptions are very widespread, because if (publicly at least) most people refuse to admit to a belief in ghosts, they nevertheless love privately to read about them.

But fiction is designed to entertain, and has its own rules of construction. A story must have plot, pace, beginning, middle, end. The events portrayed must be completely unfolded and clearly explained so that the reader may not be irritated by loose ends and unanswered questions when he arrives at the foot of the final page. Additionally, and most importantly, fiction must provide characters with whom we can identify, who can stir emotions in us, and whose morals, motives and beliefs we can fully appreciate and understand even in cases where we cannot subscribe to them.

Thus in order to conform with the rules of literary construction, the fictional ghost has become a 'stock' character — a creature whose behaviour and habits are strictly parametrized by the needs of the author and his audience. The literary ghost must be a revenant (the restless spirit of a deceased person), must have a grievance or mission that demands its haunting presence in the story, must always persistently and logically interact with the living, and above all must be instantly and absolutely recognizable for exactly what it is from the outset. Only if it fulfils all these criteria can the author succeed in building the skeleton of a workable and entertaining tale that is also acceptable to his audience.

Consequently, in the traditional ghost story the stock ghost will always seek by its behaviour to betray its supernatural origin. In this it will be ably supported by the heroine and a motley collection of servants and/or villagers (bucolic and superstitious characters to a man) whose actions and statements ('Oi wouldn't cross the 'eath after dark, Miss, not fer 'undred pound Oi wouldn't') are all designed to make the potentially dangerous nature of the revenant crystal clear to the densest of us. After a suitable interval, during which the heroine will suffer ghastly chills and horrid presentiments brought on by her frequent (but rather fruitless) encounters with the ghost, and a hapless villager or two will meet a sticky end, the intrepid hero will discover and reveal the true purpose of the revenant, including every relevant portion of its history as an incarnate being, and fulfil all its legitimate demands (justice/proper burial/murderer revealed and so forth), undergoing various strenuous and extremely nerve-racking experiences in the process. Thereafter, so as to fulfil the requirements of even the most demanding reader for a well-rounded and polished tale with a happy ending, the ghost will be shown proceeding to its well-deserved and eternal rest (another satisfied customer!), and the heroine will marry the hero — a person for whom she has probably hitherto professed an unalterable loathing.

All very nice too, but, alas, not at all true to life — or in this case, of course, death — because in the real world, ghosts, while definitely conforming to a set of rules, do not conform to those which tend to make a work of fiction a jolly good read. Indeed, far from being the wan, faded, potentially lethal and manifestly peculiar creatures fiction insists they should be, real apparitions (which are what most people actually mean when they talk about 'ghosts') are mundane, almost boring creatures. The supposed transparent lovers of darkness, defunct cemeteries and run-down residences of the aristocracy might actually be met with anywhere and at any time and have been known to walk about in full sunlight, behaving normally and politely, and looking as solid, healthy and robust as you or I. Neither, alas, do they invariably float rather than walk, and most are much more likely to enter a room quite conventionally through the door than to arrive through a convenient wall or in any other sensational manner. Nor, truth to tell, need they be the spirits of the departed — they are sometimes quite manifestly the apparition of some living person — and even when they do represent a person properly deceased, they frequently have no apparent reason for dropping in on the living. Most importantly of all, apparitions (of either the quick or the dead) are *in no way* dangerous or malicious, and it is rarely possible to discover the history of the corporeal being or to make a case for that history being causal to the apparition's appearance, even assuming that the human being it represents is safely dead to start with. Rather disappointing really, to those looking for what the Victorians so quaintly termed 'a curiosity', or for a nice healthy fright, but there you are — reality often is disappointing.

What of those people who see and believe in ghosts? Are they special, super-intelligent, spiritually highly-developed perhaps? Alas, no. They are as ordinary and unromantic as the apparitions they happen to meet. Psychic experiences of this kind are neither rare, nor confined to any particular group of people, nor dependent upon age, sex, health, levels of intelligence or financial and social status. Perhaps the most sensible comment ever made about ghosts and the people who directly experience them was made by Mrs Henry Sidgwick in her 'Notes on the Evidence, Collected by the Society [for Psychical Research] for Phantasms of the Dead', where she writes:

Perhaps the truth may be that we all have potentially the power of seeing such things, but that it requires a special state of mind, or body in us, to coincide with some external cause, and that coincidence rarely, and in the case of most individuals, never occurs.

In other words, anyone can see or experience a 'ghost' of some kind provided that they are in the right frame of mind, in the right place and at the right time. Including, of course, me — or you.

— 2 —

Definitions

Any serious dialogue on the subject of 'ghosts' must of necessity begin with a series of definitions, firstly to define the limits within which the dialogue will take place, and secondly to establish a vocabulary to enable it to take place satisfactorily.

Psychical research is a comparatively new field of endeavour (seriously commenced in 1882 with the formation of the Society for Psychical Research) and, in common with many other technical or 'special interest' subjects, it has evolved a vocabulary by means of which it might talk about itself and its interests with the greatest possible precision. It has, in fact, evolved quite specific terms by which 'ghostly' phenomena, the people who experience them, and the essential facts of such experiences might be described. Naturally this can only be to everyone's advantage. Unfortunately, however, that vocabulary is not one that allows the reader to extract meaning from context (and sometimes, regrettably, not from a dictionary either) and, really, some of the terms themselves are less than satisfactory.

The subject itself is also exceedingly broad. The kind of occurrences and experiences commonly referred to as 'ghostly' may be due to a host of causes, many of which may be interrelated and perhaps not popularly associated with 'ghosts' at all. Where, then, to begin, and where to end? Are dreams, for instance, to be included in our dialogue about 'ghosts'? They certainly have a right to be, for dreams are sometimes visions seen in sleep, and there are very many cases in which an individual has dreamed of a friend or relative and learned thereafter that person was ill or dying at the time of his dream and had some message to convey, final word to say or gesture to make. And if dreams are to be included, are the physical phenomena of the séance room to be included also? Such phenomena are, after all, 'ghostly' within the meaning of the act, as it were. The possibilities (and ergo the possibilities of confusion) are endless, and space obviously forbids the inclusion of every kind of 'ghostly' incident and the discussion of every possible type of paranormal experience.

Fortunately, careful and prolonged observation and investigation according to scientific principles has proved that 'ghostly' phenomena of any and every kind can be categorized according to the behaviour of the manifestation and the circumstances surrounding it. Furthermore, the same basic rules apply to all such phenomena. It is therefore best to begin a dialogue on 'ghostly' phenomena with an examination of apparitions, for these illustrate most clearly what the rules are, and how they work.

Apparitions are what might be called visual ghosts — ghosts that are actually seen, in other words, as opposed to those which are merely heard, touched, or sensed. The word *ghost*, however, is not a term of art in psychical research, and could not be so even were it to be applied exclusively to apparitions (which in general it is not), because it is too broad a term to be of any real use. It is sometimes used in connection with hauntings, but in the main it is witnesses rather than investigators who refer to the agent of their experiences as a 'ghost'. Effectively, however, because there is more than one kind of apparition, that word is itself not a model of precision either, being in reality a generic term (like the words *fruit* or *animal*, for example) which requires qualification if it is to be completely illustrative of the agent of a particular experience. Thus it is a word that ought invariably to be qualified by the use of additional words which define both the nature of the apparition referred to and the category to which it belongs.

Apparitions may be divided into five basic categories or types which serve to define, quite precisely and according to possible causes and/or behavioural characteristics, exactly what kind of apparition is involved. These categories are:

1. Apparitions of the living
2. Experimental cases
3. Crisis apparitions
4. Apparitions of the dead, or post-mortem apparitions
5. Ghosts, or apparitions which habitually haunt certain places.

It is important to appreciate that these divisions are in no way artificial, and exist, in fact, solely because the collation and examination of some thousands of representative cases showed that apparitions fell of themselves into such categories.

As to the vocabulary used to define apparitions, in psychical research the word *hallucination* is often used in preference to either *apparition* or *ghost*. This is, firstly, because an element of hallucination is frequently present in many (but not all) apparitional experiences and, secondly, because both *apparition* and *ghost* are quite definitely emotive terms which have become annexed to concepts which are wholly fictional, and are consequently sometimes best avoided.

Still, however, the choice remains an unfortunate one, for many doctors and psychologists persist in the belief that all hallucinations, without exception, are the result of disorders of the brain due to organic or psychological disease or narcotics of some kind. Needless to say, this is not what is meant by the word within the context of psychic research, where two separate kinds of experience — that which is *subjective* or generated entirely from within the percipient, and that which is *telepathic* and so reaches the percipient from outside himself — are described by this single term. In either case, the word simply refers to a sensory experience which seems to be normal to the percipient, but in which the physical objects experienced do not in fact come within the range of that person's normal senses. In neither case is any mental disorder of any kind implied. Nevertheless, the sense of what is really meant by the word *hallucination* is frequently lost, and this leads to inferences being drawn which are quite incompatible with the truth. Unfortunately, the word is now in common usage within its new context — albeit that the connotation of mental disorder remains indelibly imprinted upon it by virtue of its usage elsewhere — and will doubtless remain so until a better can be found to replace it.

A host of words commonplace in the literature of psychical research have, like *hallucination*, been 'stolen' from common usage and their meanings altered in this way. Some have also simply been constructed from various root words — *phantasmogenetic* is a particularly unhappy example — to fit circumstances, ideas, or events not catered for by the English language as it presently exists. In any and every case the meaning is clear and precise once one has actually grasped it, but there is no doubt that this is not always easy. Obviously a good many of these words, 'stolen' and 'tailor-made' alike, will be used in this book and, as glossaries are at best clumsy and irritating devices, such words are explained wherever they first appear in the text. *Phantasmogenetic*, incidentally, (as in a 'phantasmogenetic centre') was constructed to express the idea of 'a point in space so modified by the presence of a spirit that it becomes perceptible to persons materially present near it' and was central to a particular theory as to the possible causes of haunting.

All paranormal experiences must eventually be evaluated in not one but many ways, but initially they are adjudged either *spontaneous* or *experimental; veridical* or *delusive; subjective* or *telepathic.*

Most 'ghostly' experiences of whatever kind are *spontaneous,* that is, occurring quite by chance and sometimes without apparent reason. In nearly all such cases, the percipient (the individual who witnesses the apparition or receives telepathic information of any kind) is 'off guard' — engaged in some normal task like reading, driving or ironing which absorbs his attention or concentrates it — or else he is asleep, in which case (and particularly if the experience is telepathic, as opposed to subjective) the experience will usually be the cause of his awakening.

Where cases are not spontaneous, then they are *experimental.* In other words, there is an element of deliberation in the matter, either on the part of the agent (the apparition or individual who acts as the transmitter of telepathic information) or the percipient, or both.

Veridical experiences are those which correspond to external fact and convey information which can afterwards be verified. The criteria which determine whether a particular experience may be defined as veridical differ according to the category or type of 'ghost' concerned, and are quite specific in their requirements. Normally, if a single requirement is absent in a particular case, then the experience ought not to be termed veridical.

Experiences which are not veridical are termed *delusive.* Most dreams are delusive. Most subjective hallucinations are delusive.

Living, experimental, crisis, post-mortem, haunting; subjective or *telepathic, spontaneous* or *experimental, veridical* or *delusive*: these are the parameters within which apparitional (indeed all 'ghostly') experiences are initially evaluated. Over the course of the next five chapters, we shall be examining, one by one, each of the five types of apparition, the criteria by which they are categorized and those by which they may be adjudged veridical, by way of specific cases. We shall also look at the various experiences and feelings common to people who encounter such phenomena. Because not all 'ghosts' are experienced as visible figures, but make their presence felt by touch, sound, or a simple sense of presence, cases illustrative of this kind of experience are included too, so that it may be seen that these 'invisible visitors' fall into the same categories and abide by the same rules as their visible brethren.

Please understand that there are no 'ghost stories' in this book. Here are no neat endings, no clever and satisfying explanations of odd happenings, no classic 'B-movie' scenarios, no silly tales to set you pleasantly shivering in your chair. All of the cases used in this book are real cases, involving real people, and real 'ghosts'. Such 'ghosts' are more likely to elicit yawns than shrieks. Some of the cases referred to took place a long time ago, others quite recently. Many of them are sad, but few can be said to be in any way thrilling. None are set forth in their entirety, because space does not permit, but in every case reference is made to books or journals where a complete record may be found. No conclusions are drawn as to the possible causes of the experiences described, and in no case is any experience actually labelled veridical or delusive, subjective or telepathic. Later chapters dealing with various theories as to the nature and causation of apparitions will enable the reader to draw his own conclusions.

— 3 —

Apparitions of the Living

Apparitions of the living are exactly what they sound as though they ought to be — the apparitions of living people. About one third of all reported cases fall into this category. Living people who 'appear' as an apparition to another or others may at the time of their 'appearance' be either sleeping or waking, but their physical body will always be far from the place where their apparition is seen at the corresponding time. Often there is some evidence of physical debility and/or a state of altered consciousness on the part of the agent at the time of his appearance, and frequently an emotional link of some kind exists between agent and percipient.

Apparitions of the living may be seen by one or more persons individually or collectively, and sometimes — albeit rarely — the agent may see him or herself, the latter being variously referred to as *autoscopy* or *autophany*. Apparitions of the living usually present an appearance of absolute reality, so that percipients believe themselves to be seeing the agent of the apparition in the flesh. They may be termed veridical only if the apparition seen is that of a living person who either formerly regularly frequented the spot where the apparition is seen, or is about to arrive there (particularly if such an arrival is unexpected).

Case History No.1.
Miss Dorothy Scott.

In 1918, Miss Dorothy Scott reported as follows:

I am a nurse by profession, and at that time [1918] I was in a rather precarious state of health, due to the fact that

I had gone on working through a bad bout of influenza, and I was also terribly anaemic owing to the long-drawn-out rationing. So I was given a short holiday, and I determined to go home and take my people by surprise. I was excited about my visit, as it was a very long time since I had seen them — especially my sister Alice, who was staying there with her three children, Betty, aged 6, Jack, 3, and a baby.

My home was about 5 miles from Dunstable. This was our nearest station and I decided to walk the 5 miles over the Downs. I could walk only slowly, owing to my weak condition, and before I had accomplished half the journey I became very tired and sat down on a stone to rest. I then began to imagine what they at home would say and do when I suddenly appeared on the scene. I was in a queer, dreamy sort of state and all at once (it is difficult to explain what I mean) it seemed as though I was actually at home, and I thought I was standing in the hall looking through the half-glass door which led into the dining room at Betty and Jack, who were playing there. Jack stood and looked at me. The vision then (I should think it lasted about ten seconds) faded.

Nearly an hour later I arrived at the house and was greeted boisterously by the children, who were in the dining room at play. Jack then ran to tell his mother of my arrival. After some time had elapsed and no grown-ups had appeared on the scene, I began to feel rather hurt and went to see what had happened. When my sister saw me, she looked at me in utter astonishment and said, 'And so you really are here! When Jack came and told me just now that you had come, I said to him, "Oh no, my son, you don't take me in a second time," because, do you know, he came running to me about an hour ago very excited, and said, "Mummy, Mummy, Auntie Dolly has come." I asked, "Where is she?" and he answered that you were standing in the hall looking through the glass door. I couldn't find you and thought that you were hiding. I searched the whole place for you. Then I realised that monkey of a Jack had been playing a trick on me.' . . . I then related to her my experience on the Downs.

— *Evidence for Telepathy* by Mrs W.H. Salter,
Sidgwick & Jackson Limited, 1934.

Note that the agent admits in the first instance to physical debility and tiredness, and also that she was herself aware, whilst 'imagining' herself to be already at home, that she was in a 'queer, dreamy' state that was not quite normal to her. Note in particular her desire to be at home; that it seemed to her during the short duration of her experience that she was already at home; and that the percipient, her nephew Jack, was sufficiently convinced of her presence at that time to report it to his mother.

It might, of course, be imagined that the testimony of a three-year-old child might be suspect in such a matter, but in fact the reverse is the case. The experiences of very young children are particularly valuable simply because they are (usually!) quite unsophisticated, and therefore rarely embroider what they see or experience. In this particular case the child Jack believed that he had seen his aunt exactly where she was at that moment 'imagining' herself to be, and we can thus be assured that the apparition he perceived was both solid and convincingly lifelike. The experience was confirmed by Jack's mother, Alice, who added that Dorothy Scott was the boy's god-mother, and very attached to him.

Case History No.2.
The Hon. Henrietta Pigott-Carleton.

Early in September, 1872, I was with my father and husband at the former's shooting lodge in Co. Tyrone. An old friend, Captain M., was also staying there, and one afternoon it was arranged that I should accompany this gentleman and a keeper on a fishing expedition. My husband had some engagement, but my father walked a short way with us. He never cared to have me long away from him, and upon turning back, remarked, as he left me, 'Don't get too far from home.'

It was a brilliantly fine day; I had a book with me, and often sat down to read while the others fished. We were about four miles down the river, when, chancing to look up from my novel, I perceived a heavy cloud rising into sight above the mountains opposite. I saw we were 'in for' a drenching, thought how it would fidget my father, and wished myself at home with all my heart. In a few moments the storm burst upon us. Shelter there was next to none, and as soon as the deluge had somewhat abated, we made for the lodge, looking as though we had all been barely rescued from a watery grave. When nearly home, we were met by my father, my husband, and several men employed about the place. It seemed to me singular, not to say absurd, that my father should have turned himself and party out in such weather. Still more to my surprise, my father evidently could not get over his disturbance, spoke little that evening, and went off to bed earlier than usual.

The next day he told me that some little time after his return from the river, he sat down to read, with his back to the (western) window; that suddenly a shadow fell across the page; that, turning his head, he saw me standing at the half open window, my arms resting on the push-down sash; that he said, 'Hello! Back already!'; that I made no reply, but apparently stepped down off the low outer window sill and disappeared; that he put a mark in his book, got up, and looked out of the window; that, not seeing me, he first went to the servants and asked if I had come in at the back door; and then went out on to the little terrace before the lodge and looked around for me; that he suddenly caught sight of the coming storm cloud; that his bewilderment changed to uneasiness, and that my husband just then coming in they speedily started to search.

— *Phantasms of the Living* by E. Gurney, F.W.H. Myers
and F. Podmore, Trubner & Co, 1886, pp.531–2.

In this instance, no debility was present in the agent, but the affection between agent and percipient existed, as in the former case, together with the same urgent desire to be at home. It is worth noting, too, that Lord Dorchester not only saw his daughter some miles from her actual physical position at the time, but also saw a shadow apparently cast by her apparition. It was in fact this shadow that, falling on the pages of his book, drew his attention to his daughter's 'presence'. Neither agent nor percipient report themselves to be in anything approaching what might be called an altered state of consciousness during the course of the experience, but it is interesting that both were engaged in reading a book when the experience took place. The incidence of percipients who report that they were reading prior to experiencing a paranormal event of some kind is very high, and it would seem that the mental state induced by the act of reading therefore constitutes what was referred to in Chapter One as 'a suitable frame of mind' for this kind of perception.

Case History No.3.
Mrs L.

Mrs L. and her mother were for 15 years my most intimate friends; they were ladies of the highest intelligence, and perfectly truthful, and their story was confirmed by one of the servants; the other servant I could not trace.

Miss L., some years before I made her acquaintance, occupied much of her time in visiting the poor. One day, as she walked homewards, she felt cold and tired, and longed to be at home, warming herself at the kitchen fire. At about the minute corresponding to this wish, the two servants being in the kitchen, the door-handle was seen to turn, the door opened and in walked Miss L., and going up to the fire she held out her hands and warmed herself, and the servants saw she had a pair of green kid gloves on her hands. She suddenly disappeared before their eyes, and the two servants in great alarm went upstairs and told the mother what they had seen, including the green kid gloves. The mother feared something was wrong, but she attempted to quiet the servants by reminding them that Miss L. always wore black and never green gloves, and that therefore the 'ghost' could not have been that of her daughter.

In about half an hour the veritable Miss L. entered the house and going into the kitchen warmed herself by the fire; and she had on a pair of green kid gloves which she had bought on her way home, not being able to get a suitable black pair.

> — Letter from Dr G. Wyld in *Phantasms of the Living*
> by E.Gurney, F.W.H. Myers and F. Podmore,
> Trubner & Co, 1886, p.626.

This particular statement obviously comes second-hand, rather than directly from either the agent or the percipients — who, it will be noted, were two, thus making this a *collective* case. The statement is, however, verified by Mr W. Stainton Moses, who himself heard the story from Miss L.'s mother. Note, again, the desire to be at home evinced by the agent, who was in this instance both cold and tired, albeit quite well otherwise.

Case History No.4.
Mrs Sarah Jane Hall.

In the autumn of 1863, I was living with my husband and first baby, a child of 8 months, in a lone house, called Sibberton, near Wansford, Northamptonshire, which in by-gone days had been a church. As the weather became more wintry, a married cousin and her husband came on a visit. One night, when we were having supper, an apparition stood at the end of the sideboard. We four sat at the dining table; and yet, with great inconsistency, I stood as this ghostly visitor again, in a spotted light muslin summer dress, and without any terrible peculiarities of air or manner. We all four saw it, my husband having attracted our attention to it, saying, 'It is Sarah,' in a tone of recognition, meaning me. It at once disappeared. None of us felt any fear, it seemed too natural and familiar.

The apparition seemed utterly apart from myself and my feelings, as a picture or statue. My three relatives, who, with me, saw the apparition, are all dead; they died in about the years 1868–69.

— *Phantasms of the Living* by E. Gurney, F.W.H. Myers and F. Podmore, Trubner & Co, 1886, pp.217–18.

Very obviously this case differs in many important respects from those which preceded it, and presents very different problems of understanding. Mrs Hall was certainly emotionally linked to the three percipients, all of whom were related to her by marriage or by blood, but the idea that she was at all desirous of appearing to them and herself in her own dining-room whilst all were engaged in having supper is obviously quite ridiculous. Mrs Hall had, however, been ill some months previously, and the fact that her first child was at that time only eight months old — an age when most children still wake in the night and demand a great deal of care and attention — must also be considered as a possible contributory factor.

She had had in any event a similar experience on the occasion of her illness, when she saw herself as if 'laid out', and yet other experiences previous to that, all of which she allowed to be connected with ill-health or nervous shock. The former experiences, however, seem to have borne a greater resemblance to what is now referred to as an *OBE*, or *out-of-body experience*, than to a regular apparition of the living. Both apparitions of the living and the experimental cases discussed in the next chapter have a great deal in common with OBEs, which are not at all rare and indeed sometimes occur in conjunction with apparitional experiences. Like apparitions of the living, OBEs may also be spontaneous or experimental, and it is interesting to note that once again physical debility, tiredness or simple stress all play their part where OBEs occur spontaneously, while effort of will seems to be the primary factor when it comes to actually inducing such experiences — as indeed it does where experimental cases of apparitions are concerned. The two types of experience might therefore profitably be examined in conjunction, as one cannot help but throw light upon the other.

All this aside, however, one interesting aspect of Mrs Hall's experience remains to be considered, and it is a very puzzling one that is fraught with a great many possibilities. All the percipients, Mrs Hall included, were quite definite as to the description of the dress worn by the apparition — a light summer muslin with a pattern of spots. At the time of the experience Mrs Hall did not possess such a dress, although she wore one very like it some two years afterwards. This may, of course, be quite coincidental, but it nevertheless remains a point worthy of consideration when it comes to evaluating the case as a whole and endeavouring to arrive at a possible conclusion. Note, too, that the apparition disappeared abruptly immediately Mr Hall spoke aloud, thus disturbing the mental and physical conditions prevalent in the room at the time.

— 4 —

Experimental Cases

Similar apparitions to those defined as apparitions of the living may occur when a particular individual deliberately attempts to make his or her presence perceptible to another person or persons in a distant place. Thus the only real difference between apparitions of the living and those which are the result of experiment is that the former are spontaneous while the latter are not. The following case is a good example of an experimental case, and it will be noted that the agent, Mr J. Kirk, experienced a mild form of paralysis during the course of his experiment.

Case History No.5.
Mr J. Kirk.

On Friday, December 1st, 1882, at 9.30 p.m., I went into a room alone and sat by the fireside, and endeavoured so strongly to fix my mind upon the interior of the house at Kew . . . in which resided Miss V. and her two sisters, that I seemed to be actually in the house. During this experiment I must have fallen into a mesmeric sleep, for although I was conscious, I could not move my limbs. I did not seem to have lost the power of using them, but I could not make the effort to do so, and my hands, which lay loosely on my knees, about six inches apart, felt involuntarily drawn together and seemed to meet, although I was conscious that they did not move.

At 10.00 p.m. I regained my normal state by an effort of the will, and then took a pencil and wrote down on a sheet of note-paper the foregoing statements. When I went to bed on this same night, I determined that I would be in the front bedroom of the above-mentioned house at 12.00 p.m. and remain there until I had made my spiritual presence perceptible to the inmates of that room.

On the next day, Saturday, I went to Kew to spend the evening, and met there a married sister of Miss V. [Mrs L., whom Mr Kirk had met only once before.] In the course of conversation (although I did not think for a moment of asking her any questions on such a subject) she told me that on the previous night she had seen me distinctly on two occasions. She had spent the night at Clarence Road and had slept in the front bedroom. At about half-past nine she had seen me in the passage going from one room to another, and at 12.00 p.m., when she was wide awake, she had seen me enter the bedroom and walk around to where she was sleeping and take her hair (which is very long) into my hand. She also told me that the apparition took hold of her hand, and gazed intently into it, whereupon she spoke, saying, 'You need not look at the lines, for I have never had any trouble.' She then woke her sister, Miss V. who was sleeping with her and told her about it. After hearing this account, I took the statement, which I had written down on the previous evening, from my pocket, and showed it to some of the persons present, who were much astonished although incredulous . . . I asked Mrs L. if she was not dreaming at the time of the latter experience, but this she stoutly denied, and stated that she had forgotten what I was like, but seeing me so distinctly she recognised me at once.

— 'Report on the Census of Hallucinations' in
Proceedings of the SPR, 80c.

Note that in this case the agent was a healthy man who achieved the altered state of consciousness apparently necessary to the projection of an apparition by a living person by an effort of will. He was quite aware of his own altered state of consciousness while he was experiencing it, and he was able to describe both it and its physical results clearly and concisely. Note, also, how similar are the words used by Mr Kirk: '. . . *that I seemed to be actually in the house*' to those used by Miss Scott in Case History No.1: '. . . *it seemed as though I was actually at home*'; and how similar, too, Mrs L.'s response was to that of Miss Scott's nephew, Jack. Both percipients found the apparition recognizable and realistic, although neither had seen the agent for some time, and indeed Mrs L.

had met the agent only once before, professed to have forgotten what he looked like, and knew perfectly well that neither he nor anyone else could reasonably be in that place at that hour.

Paranormal experiences that are not completely subjective seem to be particularly vivid and memorable — indeed this is one of the ways in which telepathic experiences can be recognized. Colours seem brighter, delineation clearer, and whole figures larger than life, but sometimes the very clarity of the experience also marks it out as being in some way abnormal, or unreal. There is a case recorded, for example, where the percipient was able to read the name 'Lincoln and Bennett' very clearly inside her father's hat at a distance that would have made such a feat literally impossible without the aid of binoculars; and yet another where the percipient was able to discern the agent's dress in the sort of detail which she, being in any event short-sighted, realized herself exceeded her 'normal visual powers at a distance'. In some cases, such clarity of line and brilliance of colour may not only make the whole experience literally unforgettable, but also serve to facilitate recognition of the agent by the percipient.

The mild paralysis Kirk experienced is not uncommon in both agents and percipients, and has been reported as taking place at various stages during both experiences. Where it occurs, however, it usually lasts until the experience is over, and most percipients who report paralysis are lying down, having just woken up and observed the apparition. Sometimes, but not always, the percipient associates his paralysis with his emotional condition on perceiving the apparition, and will then usually preface his statement by saying, 'I was so frightened/astonished, etc., that . . .'

In the next case the agent also achieves his object by an effort of will, but this time the 'mesmeric' sleep of the previous case is replaced by sleep pure and simple. It should be noted that a period of intense concentration followed by sleep or a 'dream state' of some kind is an important factor in many experimental cases.

Case No.6.
F.W. Rose.

. . . Having read of cases of spirit projection, I resolved, without mentioning the fact to anyone, to endeavour to send my astral body to Mrs E. It was about 1891 or 1892, though my memory for dates is so bad that I can't be certain as to the time. This will no doubt be fixed by

others. I sat in my bedroom about half-past twelve or one o'clock and fixed my will upon the enterprise I had been considering. I carefully imagined myself going down the steps of this house, walking along the streets, arriving at S. Street, mounting to Mrs E.'s flat and going to her drawing-room and bedroom. I then went to bed with my mind fixed on the visit I wished to make, and soon fell asleep.

Nothing much happened on that occasion, save that when Mr Rose confessed to Mrs E. and her family that he had been attempting to send his 'spook' to their flat, both she and her daughter complained of a very restless night, and mentioned that the maid had been awakened by the repeated ringing of the electric bell outside her room. The bell could only be rung by Mrs E. from a button next to her bed, and she was quite sure that she had not rung it. There the matter rested, until Mr Rose decided to repeat his experiment again several weeks later. On this occasion, Mrs E. was sitting up in bed reading, and she reports her experience of Mr Rose's second experiment as follows:

Suddenly a strange creepy sensation came over me, and I felt my eyes drawn to the left-hand side of the room. I felt I must look and there distinct against the curtain was a blue luminous mist.

I could not for some time move my eyes away, and all the time I was really terrified, for I thought it was something uncanny. I wished to call my son, but fought down the feeling, knowing I should only upset him if he thought I was nervous, and possibly they would think I was going to be ill again . . . Soon the feeling of fear passed away, but all desire for sleep had also gone and for long I lay reading — when again quite suddenly came the dread and the feeling of awe.

This time I was impelled to cast my eyes downwards to the side of my bed, and there creeping upwards towards me was the same blue luminous mist. I was too terrified to move, and remember keeping my book straight up before my face as though to ward off a blow, at the same time exerting all my strength of will and determination not to be afraid — when suddenly, as if with a jerk, above the top of my book came the brow and eyes of Mr Rose. In an instant all fear left me. I dropped my book with an exclamation not complimentary, for then I knew that Mr Rose had been trying the same thing again. In one moment mist and face had gone.

— *Ghosts and Apparitions* by W.H. Salter,
G.Bell & Sons Limited, 1938.

On the following day, Mr Rose told Mrs E. and her family that he had on the previous evening concentrated all his thoughts on trying to send his astral body to the flat. The daughter then reported another restless night, Mrs E. related her experiences, and Mr Rose promised faithfully not to do it again.

Two points of interest arise here: firstly Mrs E. 'felt compelled' to look in the direction where the phenomena were focused, and secondly she was on this occasion — a very successful occasion for Mr Rose — engaged in reading a book.

The feeling of compulsion — a need to look consistently in a particular direction — often arises in cases featuring crisis or post-mortem apparitions, and its appearance in an experimental case such as this, where telepathy is definitely causal to the fact of the apparition, would seem to indicate that its reported presence in any case might be a fairly accurate means of judging whether a given experience is telepathic, rather than subjective, in nature.

Effectively, the compulsion to stare in a given direction is the result of a strong sense of presence, whether this is realized or not. The majority of 'sense of presence' cases seem to take place indoors, as this one did, and the presence is often described as being located in a quite specific position — as indeed this one was. In some cases, too, the sense of presence brings with it other knowledge, although Mrs E. does not seem to have been impressed in this way. The percipient might, for instance, feel himself able to describe the sex of the agent, or its clothing, despite the fact that he cannot see it. A sense of presence, however, frequently precedes or follows a sensory hallucination of some kind, as it did here, so that the percipient may either first feel a sense of presence and then see an apparition, hear footsteps, etc., as Mrs E. did, or first find him or herself in the presence of an apparition or other sensory phenomenon which then disappears or stops, leaving a sense of presence behind it.

The fact that Mrs E. was reading on the occasion of Mr Rose's most successful experiment is extremely interesting, as, if the state of mind induced by the activity of reading really is one of the 'ideal states' necessary to paranormal perception, this factor may have contributed largely to Mr Rose's spectacular success.

*

The next example is quite unlike the preceding two cases in this category, and is included here to illustrate the fact that the word 'experimental' is somewhat broader than it might appear to be.

Case No.7.
Lieutenant Creagh.

The passage from Bermuda to Halifax is in certain seasons hazardous, and in 1830 a transport, containing over 200 men, foundered at sea between these two ports. Two officers of the Regiment to which the detachment had belonged had, in a half-jesting way, made a sort of promise that whoever died first should come back if he could, and let the other know whether there was another world. This conversation was heard by the narrator, as it took place in his presence, perhaps a year before the events happened, though not remembered till afterwards. Liston embarked in charge of the detachment, and had been gone about a fortnight, when Creagh, who had one night left the mess early and retired to bed, and was beginning to close his eyes, saw his door open and Liston enter. Forgetting his absence, and thinking he had come to pull him out of bed (for practical joking was then more common in the army than it is now), he cried, 'No, no; d—n it, Liston, don't, old fellow! I'm tired! Be off!' But the vision came nearer the bed foot, and Creagh then saw that Liston looked as if very ill (for it was bright moonlight), and that his hair seemed wet, and hung down over his face like a drowned man's. The apparition moved its head mournfully; and when Creagh in surprise sat up, rubbed his eyes, and looked again, it was gone. Still Creagh avers that all this time he had no idea of its being a spectre, and believing that he had seen Liston himself, he went to sleep. In the morning he related the occurrence, when he recollected, but not till then, Liston's absence on duty from the Island. He asserts he had not lately been thinking of Liston, neither had the vessel been away long enough, nor had bad weather occurred to cause fears for her loss to be entertained. That he was wide awake, or at least not dreaming, is shown by his sitting up and addressing the apparition.

— *Phantasms of the Living* by E. Gurney, F.W.H. Myers and F. Podmore, Trubner & Co, 1886, Vol.II, pp.496–7.

Lt Liston was lost on the passage home from Bermuda on board the brig *Bulow* in 1831. The case was sent to Gurney, Myers and Podmore by a Mr Colchester, who extracted it from a manuscript written by his father and entitled *Reminiscences of the Bermudas*. The author of that manuscript, by then deceased, was at the time of the occurrence an assistant-surgeon in the Royal Artillery.

The authors of *Phantasms of the Living* recorded nine examples of similar compacts (which are, of course, 'experimental' in that an element of deliberation is present in the eventual appearance of the apparition) in that book, and stated that:

> ... *Considering what an extremely small number of persons make such a compact, compared with those who do not, it is difficult to resist the conclusion that its existence has a certain efficacy.*

However, they were convinced that, so far as the telepathic theory as to the causation of apparitions was concerned (a theory that will be discussed at some length in Chapter Eight), the apparent fulfilment of the compact was due to a telepathic impulse transmitted before, not after, death. The time of Lt Liston's death could not in fact be ascertained, but it is almost certain that what Creagh saw was in effect a crisis apparition that was the result of a determination to experiment. Whether such an apparition would have appeared had no specific compact been made is, of course, impossible to discover. Neither, of course, is it now possible to discover whether, and if so what, emotional tie existed between the agent and the percipient in this case (nor, indeed, in the other two cases reported in this chapter) nor whether such a tie might have been formed, or simply reinforced, by the promise made.

— 5 —

Crisis Apparitions

Crisis apparitions constitute the largest class of veridical experience. They may be caused by persons either living or dead, and must be seen, heard, felt, but most importantly recognized, by one or more persons, either individually or collectively, when the agent is undergoing a crisis if they are to qualify for this category. Once again, of course, the physical body of the agent, whether it be quick or dead, is distant from the place where the apparition is seen, and crisis apparitions usually present an appearance of absolute solidity and reality. Once again, too, there is usually some emotional tie between agent and percipient.

Crisis apparitions may be termed veridical only where:

- they represent a person known to the percipient
- they suddenly and unexpectedly appear and then suddenly and inexplicably vanish
- it is afterwards proved that the agent died or underwent any other crisis at or about the time seen, or 12 hours before or 12 hours after the time seen.

Case History No.8.
Mrs Spearman.

Eldred was greatly on my mind when baby was born, and I could only think of him. On March 19th [1917] in the late part of the morning, I was sewing and talking to baby. Joan (another child) was in the sitting room, and did not see anything. I had a great feeling I must turn round, and I did, to see Eldred. He looked so happy, and that dear mischievous look. I was so glad to see him, and told him I would just put baby in a safer place then we could talk. 'Fancy coming out here,' I said, turning round again, and was just putting my hands out to give him a hug and a kiss, but Eldred had gone. I called and looked for him. I never saw him again. At first I thought it was simply my brain, then I did think for a second something must have happened to him, and a terrible fear came over me. Then again I thought how stupid I was, and it must be my brain playing tricks, but now I know it was Eldred, and all the time in Church at baby's Christening he was there, because I felt he was and know he was, only I could not see him. All the time I thought, 'Why do I feel like this when Eldred is safe,' and Mrs K. kept telling me to look more cheerful.

— *Journal of the SPR*, Vol.XIX, 1919–20, pp.45–6.

Captain Bowyer-Bower of the Royal Flying Corps was shot down and killed in France in the early morning of 19 March 1917. He was officially reported missing, and his mother received a notice to that effect on 23 March 1917. His body was found on 10 May 1917. Mrs Spearman was his half-sister, and she was staying at an hotel in Calcutta at the time of his death. She did not know that he was out in France, because he had been at home for several months, and had only returned to France three weeks before he was killed. It was two weeks after the 19 March before she saw in the papers that he was missing in action. The date of death is confirmed by the official War Office notice, and so far as is known the captain died early in the morning. Mrs Spearman records her experience as taking place late in the morning of the same day, but allowing for the latitudinal difference between France and Calcutta, the length of time between the captain's death and his appearance to his half-sister would seem to be quite short. She did not tell anyone of her vision for almost two months, because she did not know anyone very well at the hotel (The Grand) where she was staying. Her husband was at that time away, and she did not write to him about it because 'he didn't believe in that sort of thing'.

Note that despite the fact that it would be extremely surprising to find the captain, a serving officer, at Calcutta in the spring of 1917 — particularly given the time necessary to achieve such a journey in those days — Mrs Spearman accepted his presence in her rooms as absolutely real. Note, too, that she was obviously considerably attached to her half-brother.

This case is a particularly interesting one in that there was a second verified percipient of Captain Bowyer-Bower at around this time, a small child of a little under three years old.

Case History No.9.
Betty Chater.

On 5 June 1918, Betty's mother Mrs Chater wrote:

> *One morning when I was still in bed, about 9.15 a.m. she [the child] came to my room and said, 'Uncle Alley Boy is downstairs,' and although I told her he was in France, she insisted that she had seen him. Later in the day I happened to be writing to my mother and mentioned this, not because I thought much about it, but to show that Betty still thought and spoke of her Uncle, of whom she was very fond. A few days afterwards, we found that the date my brother was missing was the date on my letter. This letter has since been destroyed.*
>
> — *Ghosts and Apparitions* by W.H. Salter,
> G. Bell & Sons Limited, 1938, pp.55–6.

'Alley Boy' had been the captain's nickname since childhood. Due to the loss of the letter it is impossible, of course, to prove the date of the child's experience, but I do not think that there is any doubt that it took place very shortly after the captain's death. Note, again, the percipient's acceptance of the apparition as a real person, and also the emotional bond between agent and percipient.

In the next case, the lapse of time between death and appearance as a crisis apparition is again very short, but here the percipient is not a relative of the agent, merely a friend and colleague. The cause of death was again related to flying, although this time the direct cause was not the result of enemy action and is effectively unknown.

Case History No.10.
Lieutenant Larkin.

> *David (M'Connel), in his flying clothes, about 11.00 a.m. went to the hangars intending to take a machine to the 'Aerial Range' for machine-gun practice. He came into the room again at 11.30 and told me that he did not go to the range, but that he was taking a 'camel' to Tadcaster drome. He said, 'I expect to get back in time for tea.*

Cheerio.' He walked out and a half a minute later, knocked at the window and asked me to hand him out his map, which he had forgotten. After I had lunch, I spent the afternoon writing letters and reading, sitting in front of the stove fire . . . I was certainly awake at the time, reading and smoking. I was sitting, as I have said, in front of the fire, the door of the room being about eight feet away at my back. I heard someone walking up the passage; the door opened with the usual noise and clatter which David always made; I heard his, 'Hello, boy!' and I turned half round in my chair and saw him standing in the doorway, half in and half out of the room, holding the door knob in his hand. He was dressed in his full flying clothes, but wearing his naval cap, there being nothing unusual in his appearance. His cap was pushed back on his head and he was smiling, as he always was when he came into the rooms and greeted us. In reply to his 'Hello, boy!' I remarked, 'Hello! Back already?' He replied, 'Yes. Got there all right, had a good trip.' I am not positively sure of the exact words he used, but he said, 'Had a good trip,' or 'Had a fine trip,' or words to that effect. I was looking at him the whole time he was speaking. He said, 'Well, cheerio!' closed the door noisily and went out. I went on with my reading and thought he had gone to visit some friends in one of the other rooms, or perhaps had gone back to the hangars for some of his flying gear, helmet, goggles etc., which he may have forgotten. I did not have a watch, so could not be sure of the time, but was certain it was between a quarter and half past three because shortly afterwards Lieut. Garner-Smith came into the room and it was a quarter to four. He said, 'I hope Mac (David) gets back early, we are going to Lincoln this evening.' I replied, 'He is back, he was in the room a few moments ago!' He said, 'Is he having tea?' and I replied that I did not think so, as he (Mac) had not changed his clothes, but that he was probably in some other room. Garner-Smith then said, 'I'll try and find him.' I then went into the room, had tea, and afterwards dressed and went to Lincoln. In the smoking room of the Albion Hotel I heard a group of officers talking, and overheard their conversation and the words 'crashed', 'Tadcaster', and 'M'Connel'. I joined them and they told me that just before they had left Srampton, word had come through that M'Connel had crashed and had been killed, taking the 'camel' to Tadcaster. At that moment I did not believe it, that he had been killed on the Tadcaster journey. My impression was that he had gone up again after I had seen him, as I felt positive that I had at 3.30. Naturally, I was eager to hear something more definite, and later in the evening I heard that he had been killed on the Tadcaster journey . . .

— Taken from a letter written by Larkin to
David M'Connel's father, 22 December 1918,
Proceedings of the SPR, 1923, 81f, p.27.

David M'Connel was a trainee pilot, aged 18, when he was killed flying an aeroplane from Srampton in Lincolnshire to Tadcaster aerodrome some 60 miles away. The accident took place in dense fog over the aerodrome at Tadcaster, and M'Connel apparently lost control of the plane, which nose-dived. The crash was seen by a young woman who ran to the plane and found M'Connel dead, and the exact time of the crash was fixed by his watch, which stopped at 3.25 p.m. Lt Garner-Smith corroborated Lt Larkin's account of their conversation, which he timed as having taken place at 3.45 p.m. The time correspondence here between death and the appearance as an apparition is therefore exceeding close — a matter of a few minutes.

Case History No.11.
Colonel H.

The Transvaal war was at its height. One night, after reading for some time in the library of the club, I had gone to my rooms late. It must have been nearly one o'clock before I turned into bed. I had slept, perhaps, some three hours or so when I awoke with a start. The grey dawn was stealing in through the windows, and the light fell sharply and distinctly on the military chest of drawers which stood at the further end of the room, and which I had carried about with me everywhere during my service. Standing by my bed, between me and the chest of drawers, I saw a figure, which, in spite of the unwonted dress — unwonted, at least, to me — and of a full black beard, I at once recognised as that of my older brother-officer. He had on the usual khaki coat, worn by officers on active service in eastern climates. A brown leather strap, which might have been the strap of his service glass, crossed his breast. A brown leather girdle, with sword attached on the left side, and revolver case on the right, passed round his waist. On his head he wore the ordinary white pith helmet of service. I noted all these particulars in the moment I started from sleep, and sat up in bed looking at him. His face was pale, but his bright black eyes shone as keenly as when, a year and a half before, they had looked on me as he stood with one foot on the hansom, bidding me adieu.

Fully impressed for the brief moment that we were stationed together at C— in Ireland or somewhere, and thinking that I was in my barrack-room, I said, 'Hallo! P., am I late for parade?' P. looked at me steadily, and replied, 'I'm shot.'

'Shot!' I exclaimed. 'Good God! How and where?'

'Through the lungs,' replied P., and as he spoke his right hand moved slowly up the breast, until the fingers rested over the right lung.

'What were you doing?' I asked.

'The General sent me forward,' he answered, and the right hand left the breast to move slowly to the front, pointing over my head to the window, and at the same time the figure melted away. I rubbed my eyes, to make sure I was not dreaming, and sprang out of bed. It was then 4.10 a.m. by the clock on my mantelpiece.'

— *Proceedings of the SPR*, Vol.V, 1888–9, pp 413–14.

Note once again that despite the manifest impossibility of the witness's brother-officer appearing in his room at his London club in the early hours of the morning while dressed as for an eastern campaign, the percipient was so impressed with the absolute reality of the figure that he doubted his own whereabouts rather than its physical presence in the room. Indeed, although he had noted the uniform worn — which was not, as he was perfectly well aware, one which would have been worn 'at home' — he still speculated that he himself might be in Ireland, serving with the man he so clearly saw before him. As will be obvious by now, however, individuals undergoing apparitional experiences quite commonly accept a very great deal that is odd, unusual, or downright peculiar on the part of their 'visitors' before it occurs to them that the events they are witnessing are at all out of the way.

Note, too, that in his statement the percipient specifically mentions colour in connection with the figure. Most reports that mention colour at all also refer to the natural appearance of the apparition, percipients being able to identify clothing and hair as being of a particular colour or shade.

A certain percentage of reports describe apparitions as being monochrome in appearance, but many of the apparitions figuring in those reports were encountered at night, or in a poor light, or were of a type where black and white clothing would have been normal to the apparition in life. Where these latter factors do not exist, however, and the apparition seen is monochromatic, percipients are usually aware from the beginning of the experience that it is a hallucinatory, or at the very least abnormal, one; and when that is so, attitudes to the apparitions seen differ quite widely from case to case, and responses are rarely of the same kind as those accorded to more 'realistic' figures. For instance, although one child was able to report meeting many times the completely black apparition of a man with a dog on a very lonely road and, while realizing the figures were 'not real' in the accepted sense, nevertheless accepted them as 'guardian angels', never experiencing any feelings of fright at all; another child of similar age, having seen a similarly black figure materialize in the bedroom he shared with his brother, formed no very favourable opinion of it, and was so frightened that he was unable to speak or cry out. (The inability to speak in the presence of an apparition is often reported, incidentally, and is usually termed *aphasia*. It is sometimes, but not always, accompanied by paralysis, and occurs for much the same reasons.)

It will be observed that in the cases of both Lt Larkin and Colonel H., the apparition not only appeared to speak, but actually took part in a more or less sensibly conducted conversation. In the case of M'Connel, really very little was said — certainly nothing that would lead the percipient to believe that anything was wrong, or that some accident had befallen the agent — and effectively the conversation was highly 'normal' in its very inconsequence. In the case of Colonel H., however, the apparition succeeded in conveying far more important information — facts, indeed, which afterwards proved to be true about events totally unknown to the percipient — but the conversation itself was almost dreamlike in its unreality, certainly far less 'normal' than that taking place between Larkin and M'Connel. Despite these differences, however, both cases qualify as examples of an extremely rare event, as in many cases apparitions appear to be either reluctant or unable to speak (see, for example, Case No.16 on page 50, relating to Miss J., and Case No.19 on page 64).

The inability or unwillingness on the part of apparitions to speak means that, in many cases, the percipient of a crisis apparition is left (like Mrs Spearman) a prey to doubt and fear until confirmation of what has occurred is received from other and more mundane sources. Oddly, this uncertainty seems less likely to occur where no apparition manifests at all, and the phenomena are of a more subtle kind. In the following two cases, for example, no apparition was actually seen, but the sensory phenomena experienced were nevertheless productive of an acute sense of certainty of disaster on the part of the percipient, which was in due course proved to be a true and accurate evaluation of events.

Case History No.12.
Mr W.B. Clegram.

I well remember a singular circumstance I have often heard my father (one of the early civil engineers of this country) relate, which occurred to himself. He was a man of very strong mind, and more free from fancies and superstitions than most people. At the time of the occurrence he was about 30 years of age.

He was in the habit of lying with his right hand extended out of bed, and one morning, about 5 o'clock, when wide awake, he felt a firm hand grasp his, so much like the grasp of his father's hand that he immediately told my mother 'that his father had taken his hand as he usually did when saying "good-bye"'. His father died at that time in the morning, somewhat suddenly. My father did not know that he was ill. His father died near Sunderland; my father at that time was living in Sussex.

— Letter of W.B. Clegram in *Phantasms of the Living* by E. Gurney, F.W.H. Myers and F. Podmore, Trubner & Co, 1886, p.574.

This is an example of an hallucination of touch that happens also to be a crisis experience, and it is interesting to note how much the mere sense of touch conveyed in this case.

Most hallucinations of touch are accompanied by other sensory hallucinations, and indeed it is quite rare that an hallucination of touch alone is reported. Most commonly, auditory phenomena either precede, or are experienced simultaneously, with the hallucination of touch, so that the percipient may hear footsteps, for instance, or the rustle of clothing, and then feel something brush against him. Where an hallucination of touch accompanies an apparition proper, it is in most cases the 'ghost' who seeks to touch the percipient, rather than the other way about, and indeed very often, if the percipient should seek to touch the apparition, contact is avoided, seemingly quite deliberately (see Case No.16 on page 50 and Case No.19, page 64).

The following is an example of a purely auditory experience, and it should be noted that despite the fact that the percipient could not identify which of his children had fallen victim to an accident, he was nevertheless sure in his own mind that one of them had and, moreover, that the accident had been a fatal one.

Case History No.13.
Mr M.P. Stephenson.

On or about the 11th November, 1882, I was awakened by two or three knocks at my bedroom door, and a voice called, 'Pa! Pa!' I called out, 'Who's there?' but no answer came. (I was sleeping alone, as my wife was ill, and slept in an adjoining room with a daughter.) At breakfast I enquired if either of them had called me; they had not done so. 'Then,' said I, 'someone else did, and I fear we shall have bad news from New Zealand,' where our two sons were living.

I awaited anxiously the arrival of the next mail, which came in the middle of December, and then we had what I believed to be the solving of the mystery. Our eldest son, on the 21st October 1882, was going to see his son at Palmerston, a town some 60 or 70 miles from Dunedin, and midway the train got off the line; some carriages were smashed. He was severely shaken, but felt nothing seriously the matter until two days after the mishap, on his return home. He was taken with cold shivering, and the doctors said they were afraid of erisipelas and blood-poisoning setting in. Such was the account of the case in our first letter. We looked with great concern for the next mail which was due on the 2nd January, 1883, although in my own mind I seemed sure he was dead; and on Christmas Day I said to a friend, who dined with us, that I believed he had been in his grave six weeks, which was the fact. The news came that my son died on the 11th of November and was buried on the 14th.

— *Phantasms of the Living* by E. Gurney, F.W.H. Myers and
F. Podmore, Trubner & Co, 1886, pp.561–2.

Mr Stephenson unfortunately did not note the time of the raps that awakened him, but thought that they occurred at about

6.00 a.m. His son died between 11.00 a.m. and 12 noon on the 11th, and if Mr Stephenson was right as to the time he heard the knocks, bearing in mind the difference in latitude, some five or six hours elapsed between the time of death and experience of the phenomena.

Quite a large number of reported cases are purely auditory in nature like this one, and by far the largest proportion of these consist of reports of footsteps or a human voice, which the percipient may or may not recognize, and which may manifest as articulate speech or as, say, a sigh or a scream. Some witnesses report sounds of human or animal activity rather than 'voices off', as it were, but in all cases, the sound seems to be localized, as it would were it a 'real' sound. Where auditory phenomena precede or accompany an apparition, they usually contribute to the realism of the overall experience, but it should be noted that sound sometimes serves only to alert the witness to the presence of an apparition, having apparently no other purpose or meaning (see Case No.18 on page 55).

Possibly the most interesting thing about auditory phenomena, though, whether they are accompanied by any other sensory hallucination or not, is their tendency to emanate from a position somewhere outside the percipient's direct line of vision — on the other side of a door, for example, or somewhere behind him. It is very rare indeed for a witness to report sounds as apparently emanating from some part of the room that he is occupying at the time, or from a spot directly before his eyes. As many witnesses display a very human and understandable disinclination to investigate the source of any unusual sound that occurs out of their direct line of vision, it is consequently unwise to assume that because the witness reports that he saw nothing, there was nothing there to be seen.

— 6 —

Apparitions of the Dead

This heading might appear to speak for itself and to be quite straightforward, but in fact it is not, because there is often some difficulty in differentiating between crisis apparitions and apparitions of the dead. This confusion arises because for some crisis apparitions the crisis *is* death, and where this is the case, some appear a little before death, some coincident with it, and yet others a little while after it.

Because one of the most important early theories as to the cause and nature of apparitions was founded upon factors relative to experimental telepathy between living persons, which proved that there is, in some cases, a slight lapse of time between the agent transmitting the idea and the percipient receiving it, the period of time elapsing between physical death and subsequent appearance as an apparition became a very important factor, and it became necessary to draw an arbitrary line defining what exactly constituted coincidence with death. Twelve hours was considered to be the maximum time reasonable to allow for deferment of receipt or realization by the percipient of the 'idea' of the agent's death, and post-mortem apparitions were thus only classified as such if the persons they represented had been dead for a minimum of 12 hours. The 12-hour period before death and the 12-hour period after it were therefore considered to be coincident with death, and apparitions perceived during these hours were — indeed, still are — considered to be crisis apparitions. Hence, of course, the stress placed on the timing of the experiences related in the previous chapter.

A post-mortem apparition is considered veridical if:

- the percipient did not know that the agent had died
- the percipient, not knowing the agent at all, was thereafter able to identify him from a photograph or by some

other means and, most importantly, the agent was previously associated with the spot where the apparition was seen
- the apparition conveys information once known to the agent in life, but previously unknown to the percipient
- the apparition manifests some characteristic, purpose, or attribute appropriate to the agent in life but unknown to, and definitely not characteristic of, the percipient.

The first case history here is a very modern one, and is taken from the book *Apparitions* by Celia Green and Charles McCreery (Hamish Hamilton, 1975). Neither the name of the percipient nor the date of the experience is given in the text, but the case was sent to the authors in response to appeals made for first-hand accounts of apparitions in 1968 and 1974 by the Institute of Psychophysical Research at Oxford.

Case History No.14.

It was Wimbledon time, and I am a tennis addict. That year I was emotionally involved with Christine Truman. On the day in question, before my daughter left for school, she prepared the laundry and, coming into the kitchen to say goodbye, she said, 'Don't forget, in your involvement with Christine, that this is laundry day: I'll leave the bundle inside the front door so that all you will have to do when the laundry man rings is sprint down the stairs, hand the bundle to him and be back in time for the next 'service'; good luck Christine.'

. . . It is relevant to mention here that, on the same floor and adjacent to our dining room, there were two other rooms both locked, each door had two Yale locks.

. . . I was 'advising' Miss Truman on tactics when I thought I heard the door bell ring; it rang again but I waited for the end of the rally.

Then I sprang from my seat, took the two short flights of stairs in two bounds, thrust the bundle into the hand of an amazed man, shut the door and got up those stairs three at a time in the hope of seeing Christine serve. As I reached the landing outside the locked door, inches from the room I was making for, [there] stood a man of some seventy years: he was dressed in a black heavy overcoat that reached to his ankles. His face was thin and swarthy, mid-Eastern in appearance, but it was his eyes that riveted my attention; they were dark, very bright but infinitely sad.

I felt no fear whatever but I experienced a deep sense of sadness and sympathy for him to such an extent that tears welled up in my eyes. After what seemed to be a long time, I made to ask him if there was anything I could do to relieve this sadness.

As I started to speak, he turned and disappeared through the double locked door only inches from where I would enter our room.

In this particular case, the percipient was able to discover that the figure she saw resembled her landlady's father, who had died in the room she was using as a dining-room some 20 years before. She also remarks that she seemed to be standing looking at the apparition 'for a long time' . . .

The question of the duration of paranormal phenomena and the human sense of time is an interesting one. Apparitional experiences vary in length in any event, but at the same time some percipients obviously realize that an alteration has taken place in the way they experience time. Certainly, apparitions may remain visible for a considerable length of time — in the case of Samuel Bull, for example, who died in 1931 and whose case is reported in the Society for Psychical Research's *Journal* for October 1932, the apparition was visible continuously for perhaps half an hour at a time. Both of the cases of haunting reported in this book (see Chapter Seven) refer to apparitions visible for similar lengths of time, but just as certainly very many experiences are of very short duration, perhaps 15 seconds or so, and yet seem very long indeed. Because of this 'relativity' it is often very difficult to establish the length in real terms of any given experience.

The second case of an apparition of the dead returns us again to Captain Bowyer-Bower, who appeared in the previous chapter as a crisis apparition.

Case History No.15.
Mrs Bowyer-Bower.

During the night, either in the late part of November or early part of December 1917, I came over very hot indeed and turned down the eiderdown, etc. Some few moments later I became extraordinarily cold with a most unnatural coldness . . . I doubled the eiderdown over myself and tried to sleep and the feeling left me slightly, but came back stronger than ever and far more intense. While I wondered what I could do a yellow-blue ray came right across the room and I at once blamed the housemaid (to myself) for not drawing the 'Raid' curtains together, thinking it was a light from the garage outside. I looked to make sure, but the curtains were well together, and as I looked the ray moved right across in front of where I lay. I watched, not at all nervously, and something like a crumpled filmy piece of chiffon unfolded, and the beautiful wavy top of Eldred's head appeared, a few seconds [later] his forehead and his lovely blue eyes came, but no mischievous twinkle, but a great intensity. It all shook and quivered, then his nose came. More waiting and quivering and then his tiny little moustache and mouth. At this point he turned his head very slightly and looked right into my face, and moistened his lips very slightly with his tongue. I kept quite quiet, but it quivered and shook so much and no chin came and in my anxiety I put out my hands and said: 'Eldred, I see you,' and it all flickered quite out, light and all.

— *Journal of the SPR, Vol.XIX, 1919–20, pp.45–6.*

Mrs Bowyer-Bower's experience raises many points of interest, not the least of which is the fact of her son's appearance, both as a crisis apparition and a post-mortem apparition, to so many different people. The captain also appeared as a post-mortem apparition, on an unspecified date, to his fiancée, who spoke to him and heard him whisper in reply. The apparition vanished upon her starting to cry. Mrs Sidgwick, who reviewed all the experiences featuring the captain, thought that it was important to consider them all together, because the fact of their occurrence could not '... but suggest some special capacity in the agent to manifest himself which could operate through various percipients and which continued after his bodily death' and, indeed, for sheer volume and variety of experience Captain Bowyer-Bower's case history stands alone.

Additionally, it will be noted that the witness mentions the sensation of cold in her statement. Sensations of cold quite unlike those experienced under normal circumstances are quite common in apparitional encounters. The feeling may occur at any stage during the experience, may or may not be localized (affecting only one part of the body), and may be attributed to the environment (i.e. a witness may say that he became aware of the sudden coldness of the room) or to the internal economy of the witness (in which case he will report that although he himself felt quite cold, he could feel, say, the heat of the fire or the sun). Most importantly, there are some indications that in some cases the sensation of cold may be subjective rather than otherwise. There is, for example, a case reported in the *Proceedings of the SPR* (Vol.VIII, 1892, p.320) involving three sisters and two maids who all stood at the doors of their respective bedrooms listening to footsteps going to and fro along the landing between them. All reported a sensation of a cold wind as the footsteps passed, but all were holding candles whose flames did not flicker, as they certainly would have done were any real current of air present in the narrow passage. (See Chapter Seven, pp. 64-83, for a complete report of this case.)

Where hallucinations are collective, the sensation of cold may be felt by one or more, but not all, of the percipients, and certainly in some cases the actual environmental temperature definitely does not alter, all of which would seem to indicate the subjectivity of the experience. It has, however, also been thought possible that the act of supernormal perception itself might bring about physiological changes which could lower the temperature of the body, primarily because a percipient in an *experimental* case mentioned a similar feeling of cold. It would therefore be unwise to dismiss the sensation as being subjective in every case.

Mrs Bowyer-Bower's description of the manifestation of this apparition as 'something like a piece of filmy chiffon' unfolding is quite unlike the way in which apparitions commonly manifest themselves — although it does bear some resemblance to the way Mrs E. experienced the apparition of Mr Rose in Case No.6 (page 30). Its vanishing suddenly and completely at the end of the experience, on the other hand, is very common indeed.

The methods apparitions use to get themselves in and out of the witness's 'reality' obviously vary from case to case, but they are most commonly first seen as a complete figure (the captain's fiancée, for example, awoke to find him sitting on her bed), with the process of manifestation a *fait accompli*. It is very unusual for a witness to be able to observe an appearance from its beginning as Mrs Bowyer-Bower did. Most witnesses, in fact, either become aware of an apparition quite suddenly — they feel compelled to turn and look at the place in which an apparition is standing, for example, or awaken and find an apparition beside the bed or elsewhere in the room — or have their attention drawn to the presence by a sound (see for example Case No.18, page 61, Carrie Miller and Miss Anderson), a sense of presence, a feeling of sudden cold or a silence around them that seems heavier than normal, and which might become quite oppressive. Sometimes, too, the apparition will enter the witness's field of vision in an entirely natural way (see Case No.17, page 51, William Stone), and it is this tendency to make the process of appearance as natural as possible that deceives so many witnesses into believing that their uninvited guest is a living person.

The same criteria do not apply, though, to the way in which apparitional experiences come to an end, for it is then rare for an apparition to leave the witness's field of vision in a natural way — although some apparitions do make sure to leave by the door, as it were. More commonly, though, at the end of an experience the apparition will simply vanish, as in this case, although in some instances it will gradually fade away, either whole, or piecemeal, from the outside toward the centre, or from the bottom up, while the percipient is still looking at it. In many cases apparitions vanish precipitately as a result of some action on the part of the percipient (the captain's mother reaching out to him and speaking, or his fiancée's weeping, or Mr Hall's speaking aloud in Case No.4, page 26), or as the result of interaction with a real object.

It is not, incidentally, particularly uncommon for a percipient to witness an incomplete apparition, and indeed the commonest type of incomplete apparition seems to be that of a head or face, as it was in Mrs Bowyer-Bower's case.

In the next case history, the apparition managed to get itself both on and off the scene in a satisfactorily normal way, but its behaviour during the course of its appearance, although, as usual, accepted without too much question by the percipient, was in fact extremely peculiar, particularly given the very rigid social code of the day, in that it appeared to be unwilling to speak, or was actually incapable of speech. Note, too, that the apparition avoided contact with the percipient, even when this was offered in such a way as to be unavoidable by a living person.

Case No.16.
Miss J.

On the evening of Saturday, April 26th, 1890, I was engaged with my sister and other friends in giving an amateur performance of the 'Antigone' at the Westminster Town Hall. A passage led down to several dressing-rooms used by ladies who were taking part in the presentation, and nowhere else. None of the public had any business down this passage; although a friend came to the door of the dressing-room once to speak to some of us.

I was passing from one dressing-room to another, a few steps further along the passage, just before going on to the stage, when I saw in the passage, leaning against the door-post of the dressing room which I had left, a Mr H., whom I had met only twice, but whom I knew well by sight, and as an acquaintance, though I had heard nothing of him for two years. I held out my hand to him, saying, 'Oh, Mr H., I am so glad to see you.' In the excitement of the moment it did not occur to me as odd that he should have come thus to the door of the dressing-room — although this would have been an unlikely thing for a mere acquaintance to do. There was a brilliant light, and I did not feel the slightest doubt as to his identity. He was a tall, singular-looking man, and used to wear a frock-coat buttoned unusually high round the throat. I just observed this coat, but noticed nothing else about him specially except his face. He was looking at me with a sad expression. When I held out my hand to him he did not take it, but shook his head slowly, without a word, and walked away down the passage — back to the entrance. I did not stop to look at him, or think over this strange conduct, being in a great hurry to finish dressing in time. Next day, as a number of us were talking over the performance, my sister called out to me, 'You will be sorry to hear that Mr H. is dead.' 'Surely not,' I exclaimed, 'for I saw him last night at the "Antigone".' It turned out that he had been dead for two days when I saw the figure.

I have never experienced any other hallucination of the senses.

— *Journal of the SPR, Vol.IV, 1889–90, p.308.*

I have included the following narrative as an extra case in this category, because it is, so far as is known, absolutely unique. Note, in particular, the very great difference in the behaviour of this apparition in comparison with that of the previous case.

Case History No.17.
Mr William H. Stone.

I think it was in 1854; at that time we were large leather factors, and hide and skin brokers in Hopstown; when I say we, my employers were in the above line of business, and I was manager of the latter department, in which we used a large amount of stationery, such as weekly catalogues, blackleads and memorandum books, etc., for our buyers and our own men. I was going along from our office, in rather a merry mood, to order from a stationer in P— Street a quantity of catalogues wanted for next Friday's sale, for we sold the hides and skins by auction every Friday, at half-past 1 o'clock to the minute, or nearly so. As I said, I was going along P— Street — it might be some six or eight days before the great St. Leger day. I generally had a pound or two on the 'Leger', and it was my intention, as soon as my little order was given for stationery, to see a friend about the horse I had backed. Crossing from right to left in P— Street, whom should I meet (or as I thought met) but an old customer, as he had been for some years, of my father's; my father was formerly a brewer, and he had supplied the party I thought I met with ale, as I said, for some years, and I used to collect the accounts from him along with many others in the same line: he was a beerhouse-keeper, or as they were called then, a jerry-shopkeeper. I went up to him, called him by his right name, shook him by the left hand, for he had no right, it having been cut off when he was a youth; he had a substitute for a hand in the shape of a hook, and he was said to be very active with this hook when his services were required in turning anybody out of his house that was in any way refractory; he was what you might call a jolly, good, even-tempered sort of a man, and much respected by his customers, most of whom did a little betting in the racing line. He had a very red countrified sort of a face, and dressed quite in a country style, with felt hat, something after the present style of billy-cocks, with a thick blue silk handkerchief and round white dots on it, his coat, a sort of cheadle-swinger, and a gold watchguard passing round his neck and over his waistcoat; his clothing was all of good material and respectably made. The moment he saw me his face shone bright, and he seemed much pleased to meet me, and I may say I felt a similar pleasure towards him. Mind, this occurred in perfect daylight, no moon-light or darkness so essential an accompaniment to ghost stories; many people were passing and repassing at the time. You may be sure I did not stand in the street for about seven minutes talking and shaking hands with myself; someone would have had a laugh at me had that been the case. I almost at once, after the stereotyped *compliments of the day, launched into the state of the odds respecting the St. Leger, and into the merits and demerits of various horses. He supplied me with what information I required, and we each went our way. He was a man considered to be well posted up in such matters, had cool judgement and discrimination; in fact, he was one of those that would not be led away by what are called tips. I made a memorandum or two, shook his hand again, and passed on about my business, ordered my catalogues, etc.*

I came back sauntering along towards the office, not now intending to see the party I had previously intended to see. As I got to the same part of P— Street, on my way back, I suddenly stood still, my whole body shook, and for the moment I tried to reason with myself. The man I had been speaking to was dead some four years before!

— 'Phantasms of the Dead' by Mrs H. Sidgwick in
Proceedings of the SPR, Vol.III, pp.83–4.

Mr Stone stood in the street for some time after this experience, turning over in his mind the possibility that his old acquaintance had suffered premature burial — something that was in the forefront of the public mind at the time — for he had seen the funeral of the publican on the day it took place, and could think of no other rational explanation that would fit the facts as he saw them. On further reflection he dismissed the idea, but remained confident that his odd meeting was a 'little mystery' that he could easily solve. Yet the 'little mystery' remained as curious to him as it now seems to us.

The tone of Mr Stone's report is lively and racy, and gives a better indication than most of the character, mind, and life-style of the man behind the pen. Perhaps because of this, I think it important to add that he insisted not only that he was quite well at the time of his experience, but that he was also quite sober, and further that he could not possibly have been deceived in the identity of the man he saw, having done business with him over a period of some years. Indeed, it would seem unlikely that he could be so deceived, if only because of the missing right hand and the presence of the hook that took its place. Interestingly, he states that he would probably not have come to the realization of the man's death when he did had he not passed again directly along P— Street and over the spot where the meeting took place. He had not thought of the man for some years.

The story is confirmed by a Mr F.A. Whaite, who at that

time ran a fine art gallery in Bridge Street in Manchester and stated that Mr Stone told him and his parents of the experience on the day it happened. Mr Whaite certainly believed it to be the truth, as Mr Stone was so excited about it at the time.

— 7 —

Haunting Apparitions

A haunting apparition, or ghost, is a figure or figures (human or animal) which is seen in the same place on a series of different occasions by one or more people alone or collectively. It may be termed veridical if:

- the percipient, not knowing the apparition at all, is thereafter able to identify it from a photograph or by some other means, and if the person represented by the apparition was previously associated with the spot where the apparition was seen
- the apparition conveys information once known to it in life, but previously unknown to the percipient.

The first case in this category was reported in the *Journal of the SPR* for November 1893 and for October 1900 (Vol.VI, 1893, pp.146–50 and Vol.IX, 1900, pp.298–306).

The three principal witnesses were sisters who were at that time living at Lessudden House, St Boswells, Roxburghshire, and the matter came to the notice of the society through the agency of a Miss E. Guthrie, who forwarded a letter written to her by Miss M.W. Scott wherein the latter described her first encounter with the apparition.

Case History No.18.
The Misses M.W., S. and L. Scott.

The first narrative of Miss M.W. Scott:

Having gone for a walk, I was returning homewards by a road in the vicinity of St. Boswells. The greater portion of the way is quite level, but at one part a short incline terminates with a sharp corner at the end. From the top of this eminence, the whole road is conspicuous, with a hedge and bank on either side. Upon reaching the specified point, and finding time limited, I thought I would expedite matters by running, and had not gone many steps when I came to a sudden halt, for just a few yards beyond I perceived a tall man dressed in black, and who walked along at a moderate pace. Fancying he would think mine an extraordinary proceeding, I finally stopped altogether to permit of his getting on further, while at the same time watching him turn the corner and pass on where his figure was still distinctly defined between the hedges referred to. He was gone in a second — there being no exit anywhere — without my having become aware of it. Greatly surprised, I then myself passed the same corner where I had seen the man vanish a few seconds before, and here, a short space onward, I saw one of my sisters standing and looking about everywhere in a bewildered manner. When I came up to her I said: 'Wherever has that man disappeared to?' and upon our comparing notes together it became evident that we had both experienced a similar sensation regarding the stranger, the only difference being that I had seen the apparition on in front, while she says he came facing her, and she, too, had noticed that he vanished almost immediately.

But here the strangest part of all is that we found that when the man became invisible to her, he appeared to me between the part of the road where she and I were standing. I may also add here that at the time we saw the apparition neither sister knew the other was so near.

Narrative of Miss Louisa Scott regarding the same occasion:

As I was walking homewards, I saw advancing towards me at an ordinary pace a tall man dressed in black, whom I believed to be a clergyman. I removed my gaze but for a second, when great was my surprise when looking up again to find that he had gone from my sight. The hedge on either side of the road is very thick, with wide fields on either side, so that the man could not possibly have sprung over it without my having seen him. I felt extremely mystified, and stood for several minutes looking backwards and forwards into the fields and in all directions, when I was much surprised by seeing my sister turn the corner of a little incline higher *up the road and commence running down it, almost immediately coming to a sudden halt, and I saw her acting in the same way as I had done about five minutes before. Soon she walked onward again, and finally turned the same sharp angle of the road and came hurriedly towards me, looking very much excited. (I had no idea that she was behind, nor did she know that I should be likely to be found in front of her.) Upon coming up to me she said, 'Where on earth is that man who was standing only about ten feet from you?' And here, what makes it more striking is that I was facing the tall spectre, and yet could not see him when my sister did. She was more fortunate than I, for she saw the entire dress of the man, while I only noticed his long black coat, the lower part of his body being to me invisible; while she had the satisfaction of seeing him entirely and also seeing him vanish, as she did not remove her eyes, as I did, from the first time of seeing him. This is all I have seen of the man, but to what I did see nothing has been added by the aid of imagination.*

Both of the above reports refer to an incident which took place on 7 May 1892 and which was timed by Louisa Scott as taking place at quarter to six in the evening.

Figure 1 is a plan of the locality and marks the relative positions of the witnesses and apparition on this and other occasions.

The same apparition appeared again some two months later, towards the end of July, to Miss Scott and another sister, Susan. On that occasion, the two women were crossing the road at the same spot when Miss Scott saw and recognized the figure as it approached her, and said, 'Oh, I do believe that is our man. I won't remove my eyes from him.' Thus forewarned, the sisters did not take their eyes off the figure, and in fact watched it until it 'seemed to fade away' into the bank on their right. The women then searched the area to see if they could see or learn anything further, but neither saw nor found anything. There were some boys on the top of a hay-cart in the opposite field at the time, who were in a good position to see much of the surrounding countryside and who certainly should have been able to see the figure when the Scott sisters did, but when questioned, they had seen no one passing on the road at all. This factor of selective visibility was to remain a constant throughout the whole length of the case as it was reported.

During the course of this last experience, Miss Scott again saw the figure complete, and was able to report that it was

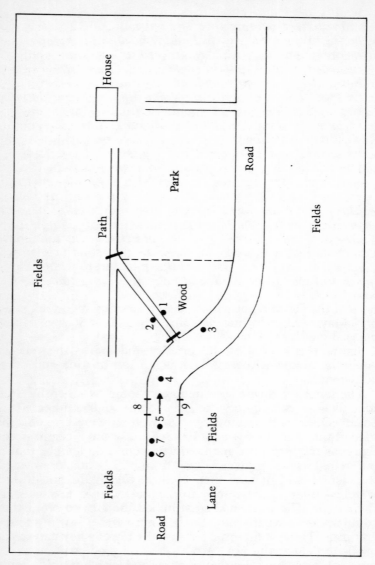

Figure 1: Plan of the locality where the Scott sisters first saw the apparition of the clergyman.

Numbers 1, 2 and 3 are respectively the positions of Miss M.W. Scott, Miss L. Scott and the clergyman in 1892.

Numbers 4 to 9 indicate positions on 16 August 1900: 4, Miss Scott; 5, apparition; 6, man on road; 7, his pony and trap; 8 and 9, gates into the fields.

wearing a long coat, gaiters, and knee breeches, all black. She remarked that its legs were very thin. Susan Scott, on the other hand, saw only the head and shoulders of the figure, and the face only in profile, and declined to give her own statement on that account, feeling that it would scarcely be worth anything. Through her sister, she described the face of the apparition as being 'exceedingly thin and deadly pale'. She thought that the man was wearing a wide white cravat and a low-crowned hat, but professed herself unable to describe the fashion. These slight differences in perception on the part of percipients who experienced the apparition were also to remain a constant factor in the reports of the case.

Miss M.W. Scott did not see the apparition again until 12 June 1893, at approximately 10.00 a.m., despite the fact that, accompanied by other members of her family and friends, she had been deliberately looking for it, travelling the same section of road over and over again in the hope of falling in with it. When it did finally appear, she was alone and not looking for it at all, and it was much further in front of her than previously. In fact, it was on this occasion at such a distance from her on the road, and so far from her mind, that she thought the figure was a real person — whether man or woman she could not tell. She thought, on drawing a little nearer, that it was a woman and, moreover, a woman that she knew, and so decided to hurry and catch up. The following is a report of her experience on that occasion:

I had not gone far, however, when I discovered it [the figure] to be none other than the apparition we had looked for and failed to see for so many months. I did not then feel at all afraid, and, hoping to get a nearer inspection, boldly followed, running in close pursuit; but here the strangest part of all is that, although he was apparently walking slowly, I could never get any closer than within a few yards, for in a moment he seemed to float or skim away. Presently he suddenly came to a standstill, and I began to feel very much afraid, and stopped also. There he was! — the tall spectre dressed as I have described before. He turned round and gazed at me with a vacant expression and the same ghastly, pallid features. I can liken him to no one I have ever seen. While I stood, he still looked at me intently for a few seconds, then resumed his former position. Moving on a few steps he again stood and looked back for the second time, finally fading from view at his usual spot by the hedge to the right.

There was no one else on the road but myself, and here I solemnly state that what I have written is not at all traded upon by imagination, as I was not thinking of the apparition at the time, he not having been seen for months previous to this visitation. With this strange experience I now felt terribly frightened, so much so that I beat a hasty retreat homewards, when further on I met a woman coming along who knew of the bad reputation of the road, and to her I related my adventure. She, too, was terrified, and declared she would go no further alone, so at last I agreed to accompany her onwards to see if we could perceive anything more of the man. We, however, reached our destination in safety, without the ghost becoming visible.

All I can say in conclusion is that I will never voluntarily pass along the same place alone . . .

Miss Scott got a very good view of what the apparition was wearing during the course of this fresh experience, and thought that it was dressed as a clergyman of the previous century in black silk stockings, shoe-buckles, short knee breeches, and a long black coat. She added that there was an old picture in the house 'for which he might have sat'.

When Miss Guthrie received this information, she was able to confirm that the dress described by Miss Scott certainly had formed a part of clerical attire at one time, as her aunt possessed a portrait of a minister in similar garb. Very usefully, she also confirmed that, having visited the locality, she was quite sure that no one could disappear from the road by the simple expedient of crawling through, or hiding himself in, the hedge, which was beech and very thick, the fields beyond being quite flat and open and giving little opportunity for concealment.

Note that on this occasion, the figure seemed to be aware of the percipient at the last, and also that it exhibited the tendency to avoid contact displayed by other apparitions of different category. It is interesting that it was the figure's suddenly stopping, and its display of apparent awareness, that seems to have frightened Miss Scott who, when earlier faced with the apparition slipping away from her, had only run the harder to catch up with it. Despite describing the figure's expression as being 'vacant', she states that it looked at her 'intently', and that having commenced walking away, turned to look at her again. This behaviour is not that of an automaton, and is quite unlike that exhibited by the apparition previously. The sensation of being personally examined is subjective but unmistakable, and it was obviously unpleasant to Miss Scott. The impression she received on this occasion proved lasting. She was never to treat the figure in so light-hearted a fashion again, although she was still to pursue it as determinedly as ever.

Enquiries as to the figure had, of course, been set in train by this time, hence Miss Scott's allusion to the 'bad reputation' of the road; but these revealed very little, save that the apparition was visible to many people, and that consequently few cared to travel that way after dark. There was a legend that the murder of a child had taken place at the spot, but there was no evidence for this, and certainly nothing of the kind had taken place within the memory of the oldest living inhabitant of the place.

First-hand evidence of previous haunting was vague, unsatisfactory, and hard to come by. Boys had seen the figure about two years before, and there were reports of blue lights being seen near the spot frequented by the apparition, but although these latter had been followed by more than one person on more than one occasion, this came to nothing, and no conclusions were drawn as to their origin, or their relationship (if any) to the apparition. Two girls (Carrie Miller and a Miss Anderson, both aged about 13) had also seen the figure whilst they were engaged in picking wild strawberries at the spot, and these witnesses were asked by Miss Scott (who interviewed Carrie Miller's mother) to give statements in writing. Unfortunately, these were never forthcoming, and this is a pity, as the apparition exhibited behaviour on that occasion which is not repeated in any of the other reports, in either preceding its manifestation, or drawing the witnesses' attention to it, by a thud or thump on the ground beside them. The girls fled immediately, but on going back some time later found the figure still standing there, whereupon it proceeded to fade away. Miss Scott apparently felt at the time that, being so young, the girls were probably unequal to the task of writing out their experiences.

A Miss Irvine, who was employed as a governess in the neighbourhood, also saw the apparition at 4.15 p.m. one spring afternoon in 1894, and her experience parallels that of Miss Scott quite closely. She was able to make a statement, but unfortunately a portion of this (the first page) has been lost, so that the only complete record of her experience now remaining is that given by Miss Scott, who wrote to Miss Guthrie about it on 14 August 1894. According to Miss Scott, this witness saw what she described as a tall old man in front of her as she was returning home along the haunted road:

My informant was much interested in this peculiar looking person, and did not take her eyes off him, whilst she watched him walk backward and forward between the turn of the road and a heap of stones about an hundred yards lower down; he repeated this six times, the last time stopping as if he were speaking to a man who was cutting the hedge at the time. What struck Miss Irvine as peculiar was that the man who was hedge-cutting did not look round, and seemed quite unconscious of the other's presence. Miss Irvine walked on, and was going to pass the old man, when, to her astonishment, he vanished when she was only about three yards from him. I know you will think it foolish of Miss Irvine not questioning the hedger to whom the apparition looked as if he were speaking. I asked her why she had not, and she answered that she had not liked doing so, as the labourer would undoubtedly have thought her mad, as he clearly did not see anyone.

The second, surviving, page of Miss Irvine's own statement contains a description of the apparition which tallies with that of Miss Scott in every respect save that Miss Irvine thought the figure wore a long black cloak with a cape. Miss Irvine did state, however, like everyone else who saw the figure, that it was dressed 'rather like a clergyman'. She was apparently much upset by her experience, going into a nearby house for comfort, where she 'took hysterics', according to Miss Scott.

The apparition continued to appear for some time after, and was still being seen in 1900. Miss Scott saw it on several other occasions, and it is interesting to note that in August 1898 she reported that she had heard footsteps walking beside her on the road, but saw nothing, feeling only a sense of presence:

. . . when coming down the haunted road in the dusk I distinctly heard footsteps walking beside me, but could see nothing, though I am sure there must have been an unseen presence around from the state of nervous terror which generally makes itself felt on such occasions.

It is also interesting that this report would seem to indicate that she had experienced the phenomena in this form more than once, and worth remembering, too, that on more than one occasion the apparition was visible to her, but not to the person who was with her or in the near vicinity — an effect common to both of the cases set out in this chapter. Miss

Scott, however, was less reticent than the governess, and we are therefore assured that on the occasion of 16 August 1900 the figure really was visible to no one but herself:

> *There was a man with a pony and trap cutting grass by the roadside, within a few feet of where I saw the apparition appear, who had his back to the worker; yet, the most wonderful part of it all is that when I questioned the man, he declared he had seen 'no one'.*

In fact, it was the pony, rather than the man, who was nearest the apparition, and Miss Scott reports that it 'gave a violent shake of its harness' at the time. She very fairly points out, however, that horses 'frequently go through such antics for other causes' and that the animal's reaction could be 'no criterion for judging the point'.

In the same way, the apparition also proved invisible to Louisa Scott in the autumn of 1897, when it walked alongside her and Miss M.W. Scott, 'within three feet' of the latter and quite visible to her. On that occasion Miss Scott remarked, 'This ghost always appears when our thoughts are bound up in something else, but if the opposite, then we are sure not to see him, and many persons who have accompanied us up [and] down the road in the hopes of seeing him have, like ourselves, failed to do so . . .' This is another effect common to experiences of this type, which very adequately bears out Mrs Sidgwick's remarks as to the right state of mind being necessary to such experiences.

Here the report in the *Journal* ends, but in October 1900 Miss Scott wrote to the society in acknowledgement of some copies of that publication sent to her, adding that she had heard further reports of the 'ghost' from two step-sisters, one of whom kept the lodge at Lessudden House. The lodge-keeper's experience had taken place some six years previously, when she had seen the figure off the road 'beyond the church'; but her step-sister's experience was more recent and very much more in keeping with the main body of reported sitings. She had seen the figure in twilight when she was returning home from a nearby village after attending a mothers' meeting. When she arrived at the haunted road, the figure was already on it, just in front of her, and for some time they walked almost together. Eventually she passed it, but was so much frightened by that time that she continued her journey home by the shortest route across the fields to get away from it. She said that the figure was 'so light of foot he made no sound in walking'.

Miss Scott also wrote that she had 'by the merest chance' heard the story of the apparition, the ghost being believed to be that of a clergyman in St Boswells who had murdered his servant. She went on to say, 'It must have taken place quite 150 years ago as we can trace the ministers of the parish back to a certain date without a blot on their escutcheons.' She intended to try to find out more about the story she had been told, because she felt certain in her own mind that it was true, but there is no record that she ever did so, so that evidence as to the truth of the story remains poor and inconclusive.

Miss Scott's assumption, which obviously practically amounted to a certainty, that the apparition was the result of, or associated with, a tragedy or a crime, may have been based upon subjective feelings of which we know nothing, but it is equally possibly quite without foundation. The agent of the apparition may well have been deeply unhappy, or in considerable pain, or simply in the habit of walking the road in life for reasons known only to himself. A tragedy or a crime is not a prerequisite to the appearance of an apparition of this or any other type — although, as we have seen, agony of mind or the need to be in touch with another person is sometimes a predisposing factor.

Case History No.19.
Miss R.C. Despard.

This very famous case of haunting centred about a house which stands at the corner of Pittville Circus Road and All Saints Road, Cheltenham. The house was originally called 'Garden Reach', and was built in about 1860 on the site of a market garden. It had quite a large garden and an orchard, and was first inhabited by Henry Swinhoe, a solicitor, who bought it from the builders and lived there with his wife Elizabeth until she died on 11 August 1866, aged 35. Henry married again in February 1870, and continued to inhabit the house with his second wife, Imogen. He died in July 1876, Imogen having left him and moved to Clifton, near Bristol, a few months before. She herself died, aged 41, in September 1878, still living at Clifton, and having never entered the house at Cheltenham after she left it some two years before. Her body, however, was returned to the town, and she is buried at Holy Trinity Church, Portland Street, some 500 yards from her former home.

On Henry Swinhoe's death, 'Garden Reach' was sold to a Mr

Littlewood, an elderly gentleman who lived there with his wife. The couple had two sons, who visited them from time to time, but never stayed for long periods. The house was in a rather dirty condition when Mr Littlewood took it, and needed to be thoroughly done up. The new owner, however, having changed the name of the house to 'Pittville Hall', died within six months of going into it (by coincidence, in the same sitting-room where Mr Swinhoe had also died), and his wife soon after moved to a smaller house nearby. 'Pittville Hall' then remained empty more or less consecutively for some four years until it was rented by Captain Despard, who immediately changed its name to 'Donore'. According to the narrator of the story, Rosina Despard, who was at that time 19 years old, the house was then considered to be a typical modern detached residence and was in good repair. Nothing had been heard of its being haunted.

Figures 2, 3 and 4 show a plan of the house. A further plan was drawn by B. Abdy Collins in 1946 (Figures 5 and 6), showing several alterations and additions to the house as it would have been in Miss Despard's time. A chapel had been built on the All Saints Road side of the house, and a covered way constructed from the garden door to a series of outside rooms intended for the use of visitors. However, the interior of the house in 1946 was much the same as it was when it was built, the only real change being that the drawing-room had been partitioned. It is therefore possible to show the usual route taken by the apparition with some accuracy.

Miss Despard lived at 'Donore' with her father, Captain F.W. Despard, her mother (who was an invalid), three sisters (Edith, Lillian and Mabel, then 18, 15 and 13 respectively) and two brothers (Henry and Wilfred, aged respectively 16 and 6), the elder of whom was away most of the time at school. There was another, married, sister, a Mrs Kinloch, who visited the house frequently, sometimes with her husband, but more often without him.

The family moved into the house in April 1882, and nothing was seen there until the following June, when Rosina Despard saw the apparition of a woman on the landing outside her bedroom door. Miss Despard's account of the haunting originally formed part of a series of letters she wrote to Catherine Campbell, a friend, but Miss Campbell refused to give these up, as they referred to other matters of a private nature. It is not now known where those letters are, if they still exist, and the present account was written out by Miss Despard for the Society for Psychical Research and appeared in the *Proceedings* of the society under the title 'Record of a Haunted House'

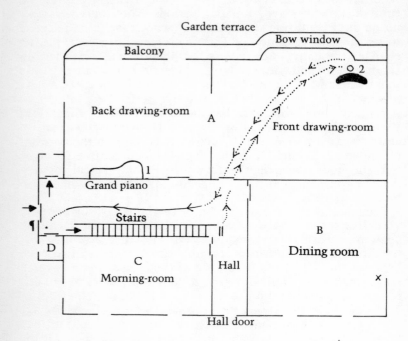

Figure 2: Plan of the Ground Floor.
The two drawing-rooms are separated by a wide archway formerly filled by folding doors.

1. Position of the music stool, sitting on which Edith Despard saw figure behind her on 12 August 1884.

2. Sofa on which the figure sat, the dot marking the position behind, which it took up when the sofa was occupied.

* Marks the spot where the figure usually disappeared.

‖ Marks the position of the mat.

.... Marks the usual track of the figure when it was followed downstairs, into the drawing-room and along the passage to the garden door, where it disappeared.

× Window looking onto the orchard.

¶ Garden door by which the figure disappeared.

→ Shows the direction in which doors open.

D A small lobby from which stairs go down to the basement and a servants' staircase leads up to a half-landing between the ground and first floors.

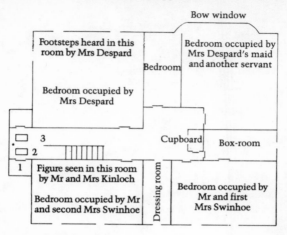

Figure 3: Plan of the First Floor.
* Half-landing between the ground floor and the first floor.
1. Door opening from the servants' staircase.
2. Stairs from the ground floor.
3. Stairs up to the second floor.

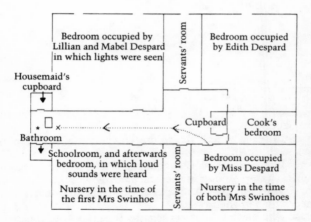

Figure 4: Plan of the Second Floor.
   * Half-landing between the first and second floors.
   × Marks the position of the figure when first seen by Miss Despard.
   .... Marks the course from Miss Despard's bedroom door to the head of the stairs, where the figure usually paused, looking towards the bathroom door, before continuing straight down the stairs, not stopping on the first floor, and on the ground floor pursuing the course marked.

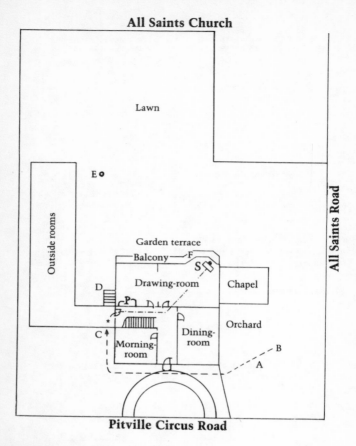

Figure 5: The Grounds.

A   Approximate place where the figure was seen by the General from across the road.

B–C Line taken by the ghost on 12 August 1884.

D   Steps down to the kitchen in the basement where the ghost was seen that same evening. Also the spot where the charwoman was standing when she saw it.

E   Stone vase where the figure was seen by the cook.

F   Balcony where the gardener saw the figure at 6 a.m. in August.

P   Position of the music stool, sitting on which Edith Despard saw the figure behind her on 12 August 1884.

S.   Sofa on which the figure sat, the dot marking the position behind, which it took up when the sofa was occupied.

–·– Marks the usual track of the figure when it was followed downstairs, into the drawing-room and along the passage to the garden door, where it disappeared, usually at *.

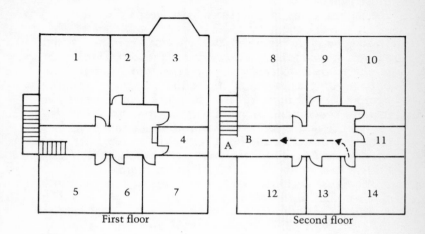

Figure 6: The First and Second Floors.

1. Footsteps heard in this room by Mrs Despard. Bedroom occupied by Mrs Despard.
2. Bedroom.
3. Bedroom occupied by Mrs Despard's maid and another servant.
4. Box-room.
5. Figure seen in this room by Mr and Mrs Kinloch. Bedroom occupied by Mr and the second Mrs Swinhoe.
6. Dressing room.
7. Bedroom occupied by Mr and the first Mrs Swinhoe.
8. Bedroom occupied by Lillian and Mabel Despard, in which lights were seen.
9. Servants' room.
10. Bedroom occupied by Edith Despard.
11. Cook's bedroom.
12. Schoolroom, afterwards a bedroom, in which loud sounds were heard.
13. Servants' room.
14. Bedroom occupied by Miss Despard. Nursery in the time of both Mrs Swinhoes.
A Half-landing between the first and second floors.
B Marks the position of the figure when first seen by Miss Despard.
— — — Marks the course from Miss Despard's bedroom door to the head of the stairs, where the figure usually paused, looking towards the bathroom door, before continuing straight down the stairs, not stopping on the first floor, and on the ground floor pursuing the course marked.

(1892, Vol.8). The case was also discussed in the *SPR Proceedings*, 1885. Miss Despard was referred to as Miss R.C. Morton in those papers.

The report begins in June 1882. Miss Despard writes:

> *I had gone up to my room, but was not yet in bed, when I heard someone at the door, and went to it, thinking it might be my mother. On opening the door, I saw no one; but on going a few steps along the passage, I saw the figure of a tall lady, dressed in black, standing at the head of the stairs. After a few moments she descended the stairs, and I followed for a short distance, feeling curious what it could be. I had only a small piece of candle, and it suddenly burnt itself out; and being unable to see more, I went back to my room.*
>
> *The figure was that of a tall lady, dressed in black of a soft woollen material, judging from the slight sound in moving. The face was hidden by a handkerchief held in the right hand. This is all I noticed then; but on further occasions, when I was able to observe her more closely, I saw the upper part of the left side of the forehead, and a little of the hair above. Her left hand was hidden by her sleeve and a fold of her dress. As she held it down a portion of a widow's cuff was visible on both wrists, so that the whole impression was that of a lady in widow's weeds. There was no cap on the head but a general effect of blackness suggests a bonnet, with a long veil or a hood.*

This was Miss Despard's first encounter with the ghost, but over the next two years she saw it on perhaps half a dozen further occasions. During this time she mentioned it, however, only to Miss Campbell, who never spoke of it to anyone else, so that the rest of the Despard family were unaware that she had experienced anything at all in the house. Nevertheless, during the same two-year period, the apparition was seen three times by other people: by Miss Despard's sister Mrs Kinloch in 1882, by a housemaid (unnamed) in the autumn of 1883, and in the drawing-room the same year by Wilfred Despard and another little boy.

Mrs Kinloch saw the figure on the stairs at about half-past six in the evening (when it was apparently still quite light), but assumed that it was a Sister of Mercy calling at the house and thought no more about it. The housemaid, however, saw it at 10 o'clock in the evening, and was so convinced of its being a living person that she thought that someone had got into the house, insisting that the premises be searched for intruders. Her description agreed closely with what Miss Despard had seen, but as on searching no one was found, her story received no credit. The little boys were playing on the terrace and spotted the figure through the drawing-room window. It is interesting that they were obviously able to hear the figure also, since they ran into the house because it was weeping so bitterly. They found no one in the drawing room, however, and were told by the parlour-maid that no one had called.

Several times Miss Despard followed the figure down the stairs and into the drawing-room, where it would remain for a time before going along the passage towards the garden door, at which point it invariably disappeared. On 29 January 1884, however, she decided to speak to the figure for the first time:

> *I opened the drawing room door softly and went in, standing just by it. She came in past me and walked to the sofa and stood still there, so I went up to her and asked if I could help her. She moved, and I thought she was going to speak but she only gave a slight gasp and moved towards the door. Just by the door I spoke to her again, but she seemed as if she were quite unable to speak. She walked into the hall, then by the side door she seemed to disappear as before.*

Note that, as with Miss Scott in the previous report, the apparition seemed to be aware of the percipient on this occasion, and also that it seemed to want to communicate, although it was unable to do so. Unlike Miss Scott, however, Miss Despard records no unpleasant or uncomfortable sensations in respect of this, or any other, of her experiences with the ghost, saying only:

> *. . . as to the feelings aroused by the presence of the figure, it is very difficult to describe them; on the first few occasions, I think the feeling of awe at something unknown, mixed with a strong desire to know more about it, predominated. Later, when I was able to analyse my feelings more closely, and the first novelty had gone off, I felt conscious of a feeling of loss, as if I had lost power to the figure.*
>
> *Most of the other percipients speak of feeling a cold wind, but I myself have not experienced this.*

The family's dogs, however, reacted rather differently, one in particular several times greeting the apparition as though it were a living human being, and then retreating dismayed under the sofa. The Despards also kept a cat, but it lived mostly in the kitchen, and no one noticed anything peculiar about its behaviour at all, despite the fact that the apparition was seen on more than one occasion on the kitchen steps.

In May and June 1884, Miss Despard began experimenting with the apparition, tying strings with marine glue on them across the stairs at varying heights from the ground, and attempting to touch the figure. Nothing came of this. The figure drifted through the strings, leaving them intact, and characteristically avoided being touched or confined. Rosina reported, 'It was not that there was nothing there to touch, but that she always seemed to be beyond me, and if followed into a corner, simply disappeared.' Again, the resemblance to Miss Scott's experience is marked, the figure seeming to skim away, to be always just beyond the reach of the percipient.

At first the intervals between one appearance and another were quite long, but these grew shorter as time went on, and it became apparent that the appearances were always more frequent during the months of July, August, and September, or those months in which the deaths of the various members of the Swinhoe family had taken place. The only noises heard during the first two years, too, were trifling: slight pushes against Miss Despard's bedroom door accompanied by footsteps — these being very light but recognizably those of the apparition. 'Her footstep,' wrote Miss Despard, 'is very light, you can hardly hear it, except on the linoleum, and then only like a person walking softly with thin boots on.' This state of affairs, however, was not to continue, and during July and August 1884, the appearances reached a peak:

July 21st: I went into the drawing room, where my father and sisters were sitting, about 9 in the evening, and sat down on a couch close to the bow window. A few minutes after, as I sat reading, I saw the figure come in at the open door, cross the room and take up a position close behind the couch where I was. I was astonished that no one else in the room saw her [neither Captain nor Mrs Despard ever saw the apparition], as she was so very distinct to me. My youngest brother, who had before seen her, was not in the room. She stood behind the couch for about half an hour, and then as usual walked to the door. I went after her, on the excuse of getting a book, and saw her pass along the hall, until she came to

*the garden door, where she disappeared. I spoke to her
as she passed the foot of the stairs, but she did not
answer, although as before she stopped and seemed as
though about to speak.*

Note that yet again, the apparition seemed to show awareness
of Miss Despard when spoken to, and seemed to wish to reply.
Note too, that the visibility of the figure is selective, as in the
previous case, being visible in this instance to only one of
several people present.

On 31 July, Edith Despard saw the figure when it passed her
on the stairs. She had been downstairs talking to another
sister, and was disturbed enough about the experience to go to
Rosina's room to tell her of it. On that occasion Rosina tried
to pass it off as one of the servants, but in fact found that none
of them had been out of their rooms at the time. Edith's
description of the woman she saw tallied in any event with
what Rosina had herself seen. Rosina saw the figure again on
1 August. She had heard footsteps outside her bedroom door
and opened it in time to see the apparition at the end of the
landing at the top of the stairs. She again followed it along
what had now become a familiar route — down the hall, into
the drawing-room to the bow window where the figure stood a
while, out of the room and down the passage to the garden
door and the final disappearance. She again spoke to it without
response.

By 2 August, most of the household were aware of the
presence of the apparition, the footsteps being heard by all
three of Miss Despard's unmarried sisters, by the cook (who
slept on the top landing), and also by Mrs Kinloch, who was
sleeping on the floor below. None of them would go out on
the landing after hearing them pass, but all stated that they
had plainly heard them passing and repassing outside their
doors, and all described them as being unmistakable — 'soft
and rather slow, though decided and even'. On being questioned as to whether any of the servants had been out of bed
the night before, the cook said that they had not, but admitted
to having heard the footsteps before, and to having seen the
apparition on the stairs one night, and also on the terrace walk
at about 11 o'clock one morning. Her description of the figure
matched that seen by Miss Despard. Unfortunately, no statement was ever taken from the cook, as she left the Despards'
employ when her mother died, and could not afterwards be
traced.

On 5 August, Miss Despard told her father what had been
seen and heard. He was astonished, neither he nor Mrs Despard

ever having seen anything at all, and immediately made enquiries of the landlord, who had lived some months in the house himself. The landlord (very naturally, all things considered!) replied that he had never seen anything unusual in or around the house, despite the fact that he himself had lived in it for a short time.

On 6 August a neighbour, General Annesley, sent his son to enquire after Mrs Kinloch, who was then in mourning for a baby son, because he had seen a lady crying in the orchard. He described her as being tall, dressed in black, wearing a bonnet with a long black veil, and a handkerchief held up to her face. Miss Despard remarked that this was the second time the figure had been mistaken for that of a real person, the outline being very distinct, and the whole appearance solid. General Annesley came over that evening, and the whole group took up stations to watch for the ghost, but it never came, although footsteps were heard by Mrs Kinloch and her husband going up and down the stairs later on. The general (who was a friend of the landlord) was later to say that he had no recollection of seeing the figure at all, nor of forming a party to watch for it.

On 11 August, both Rosina Despard and Mrs Kinloch saw the figure standing on the balcony looking in at the drawing-room window. It stood there for some moments, and then walked to the end and back again and disappeared. Later the same evening it once again took up its station in the drawing-room, but at that time only Miss Despard saw it, while Mrs Kinloch, who was also present, did not.

On the evening of 12 August, Rosina Despard was in the orchard when she saw the figure pass through it, along the sweep at the front of the house, and in through the open side-door, whereupon it made its way across the hall and into the drawing-room to take up its usual position behind the couch in the bow window. Rosina followed, and when her father entered the drawing-room a short time afterwards she pointed the figure out to him. He could not see it, but following his daughter's directions went up to where it was standing. Once again, the figure avoided contact, oddly seeming to show at least a sort of awareness of a person who was not himself aware of it. It moved swiftly around behind him and out of the room, disappearing as usual by the garden door. Both Rosina and Captain Despard went out into the garden to look for the figure, first having to unlock the door, which the captain had locked as he came in, but saw nothing of it.

Later that evening, however, the figure reappeared. Edith found it standing behind her in the back drawing-room where she was playing the piano, bending over her as though to turn over the sheets of her music. She felt a cold icy shiver on that occasion, which drew her attention to the presence of the figure, and immediately went to call her sister Rosina, who on entering the room said that she could see the figure standing in its usual position by the bow window, although it was by then invisible to Edith. Rosina spoke to it then several times, but without response, although it continued to stand there for some 10 or 15 minutes before going out and disappearing as usual by the garden door.

Mabel Despard, just then coming in from the garden, said that she had seen the figure coming up the kitchen steps outside. All three sisters went out into the garden, and on seeing them there, Mrs Kinloch called out from a first-floor window that she had just seen the figure pass along the lawn in front, and down the carriage drive towards the orchard. Altogether that evening then, some four people saw the apparition, either alone or collectively.

On the morning of 14 August, the parlour-maid saw the figure in the dining-room at about 8.30. The family made arrangements to watch that evening, but, characteristically, saw nothing. The parlour-maid was later interviewed by Frederick Myers, and gave her own account of the experience.

On 16 August, Miss Despard again saw the figure outside on the balcony, but it did not come into the room afterwards, as it had previously. The gardener reported, however, that he had seen it in the same place at 6.00 a.m. that morning. Three days later, the whole family went on holiday for a month, leaving three servants to look after the house. The servants reported hearing frequent noises during their absence, but Miss Despard was inclined to put much of this down to the fact that the stair-carpets were up for part of that time, and the house empty. The cook, however, reported seeing the figure standing by a stone vase in the garden.

During the remainder of 1884 and the whole of 1885, the figure continued to be seen in exactly the same way, in the same places, and particularly in the months of July, August, and September, by various people. The footsteps continued, and were heard by several visitors as well as by new servants who took the place of those who left. Soon, too, other sounds began to be heard, and these seemed gradually to increase in intensity: footsteps on the second-floor landing; bumps against the bedroom doors; door-handles turning; new footsteps, heavy and irregular, lasting through the greater part of the night, and being heard three or four times a week. There were similar noises on the first-floor landing, particularly in the front right-hand room, which was that formerly used by Henry and

Imogen Swinhoe, and in the summer of 1885, very heavy thuds and bumpings were heard, especially on the upper landing.

During 1885, Miss Despard kept a camera handy, at Frederick Myers' suggestion, in order to try to photograph the figure. She had no success. She also attempted consistently to communicate with it, by speech and sign language, again without result. She again tried to touch the figure, but failed, despite having cornered it twice.

In July 1886, while Captain Despard was away:

> . . . *my mother and her maid heard a loud noise in an unoccupied room over their heads. They went up, but seeing nothing and the noise ceasing, they went back to my mother's room on the first storey. Then they heard loud noises from the morning room on the ground floor. They then went half way downstairs, when they saw a bright light in the hall beneath. Being alarmed, they went up to my sister Edith, who then came down, and they all three examined the doors, windows, etc., and found them all fastened as usual. My mother and her maid then went to bed. My sister Edith went up to her room on the second storey, but as she passed the room where my two sisters Lillian and Mabel were sleeping they opened their door to say that they had heard noises, and also seen what they described as the flame of a candle, without candle or hand visible, cross the room diagonally from corner to door. Two of the maids opened the doors of their two bedrooms, and said that they had also heard noises; they all five stood at their doors with their lighted candles for some little time. They all heard steps walking up and down the landing between them; as they passed they felt a sensation which they described as 'a cold wind', though their candles were not blown about. They saw nothing. The steps then descended the stairs, reascended, again descended, and did not return.*

It should particularly be noted that Mrs Despard never saw, and rarely experienced, any of the phenomena in the house. It is interesting and very germane, too, in view of the nature of this specific experience, that Mrs Despard was rather deaf.

During the autumn of 1886 the family began to hear rumours of earlier haunting of the house. They made extensive enquiries, and although they had difficulty in obtaining first-hand accounts of events on the premises prior to their own occupation, it is at about this time that the apparition began to be identified with the second Mrs Swinhoe. Miss Despard made a list of the reasons for connecting the figure with Imogen:

1. The complete history of the house is known, and if we are to connect the figure with any of the previous occupants, she is the only person who in any way resembled the figure.
2. The widow's garb excludes the first Mrs Swinhoe.
3. Although none of us had ever seen the second Mrs Swinhoe, several people who had known her identified her from our description. On being shown a photo-album containing a number of portraits, I picked out one of her sister as being most like the figure, and was afterwards told that the sisters were much alike.
4. Her step-daughter and others told us that she specially used the front drawing-room in which she continually appeared and that her habitual seat was on a couch placed in a similar position to ours.
5. The figure is undoubtedly connected with the house, none of the percipients having seen it anywhere else, nor had any other hallucination.

This identification of the apparition as Imogen Swinhoe has led, over a period of years, to the uncovering of a great deal about the Swinhoes and their life together.

During the course of their investigations, the Despards heard from a carpenter who had done various jobs for the Swinhoe family, including making a receptacle under the floor of the morning room that was designed to hold Elizabeth Swinhoe's jewellery. The jobbing carpenter told the Despards that Henry Swinhoe had told him that Imogen wished to possess herself of her predecessor's jewellery, and that he had himself watched Henry Swinhoe place the jewellery in the receptacle he had made, and had afterwards nailed down the boards and replaced the carpet for him. The carpenter had never experienced anything untoward in the house, and the morning room was a room in which the apparition was never seen, but the receptacle and its avowed purpose throws an interesting light on the relationship existing between Henry and Imogen at that time, and also provides important contributory evidence to statements made by other people, although it must be said that these are often contradictory or conflicting.

Henry Swinhoe is reported by Rosina Despard to have been passionately fond of his first wife, and to have begun drinking heavily after her death. According to this version of the tale — and Miss Despard does not tell us from whom she heard it, although the fact that she reports it at all probably indicates that it was current in the neighbourhood at the time — the second Mrs Swinhoe 'was in hopes of curing him of his intemperate habits', but instead took to drinking herself. Quite a different story, however, was given to Andrew Mackenzie by Mr Swinhoe's grand-daughter, who said that Henry Swinhoe had discovered on his honeymoon that Imogen was a heavy drinker, and that it was because of this that he himself took to drinking (*Hauntings and Apparitions*, Andrew Mackenzie, Paladin Press, 1983, pp.47–74).

The truth probably lies somewhere between these two diametrically opposed points of view, with faults attributable to both Henry and Imogen, but all sources agree that the marriage was not a happy one, 'embittered by constant quarrels, frequently resulting in violent scenes', and that the primary subjects of dispute between the parties were the management of the children, Mrs Elizabeth Swinhoe, and the possession of that lady's jewellery. Henry Swinhoe's grand-daughter stated that the children endured 'years of tyranny and misery under Imogen'. Rosina Despard, who obviously spoke to at least one of the children, does not mention this at all — although she may have known, or at least had an inkling, of it — but she does say that the purpose of the receptacle was 'to preserve' the jewellery for them.

As the jewellery was so obviously a bone of contention between the couple, matters having reached such a pass that Henry saw fit to employ someone to hide it from his wife, Captain Despard had the carpenter take up the boards, in case it should still be in the house. Sure enough the receptacle was there, but it was empty. The boards were also taken up near the garden door where the figure was seen to disappear so regularly, but there was nothing there either, and it was obvious from the state of the cavity revealed that nothing ever had been there.

Captain Despard next went to Bristol to look at the Register of Births and Deaths. He found that the cause of Imogen Swinhoe's death was given as dipsomania and intervening sub-gastritis. He also called on the doctor who had attended Mrs Swinhoe to ask whether there had been any disfigurement of the face which would account for its persistent concealment. There had not, although, he was told, the face had become more full and round.

From the Despards' point of view, the haunting at this point begins to run down. During the years 1887 to 1889 the figure was seen very seldom, and from 1889 to 1892 it was not, so far as Rosina Despard could ascertain, seen at all. She also remarks that the figure became less substantial as time went on, and that its upper part always made a more distinct impression than the lower, although this, she added, could be due to the fact that 'one naturally looks at people's faces before their feet'. At all times, however, the figure intercepted the light, although the family were not able to ascertain whether or not it cast any shadow.

The Despard family left the house in 1893, but some 50 years after the publication of 'Record of a Haunted House' a Mr George Gooding wrote to the SPR to say:

> I will gladly give you any information I can, but I fear it is very meagre, though perhaps slight confirmation of what must be already on record ... My main difficulty is to separate clearly in my mind my own actual experience from knowledge acquired at the time or subsequently from older friends or other sources. It must be remembered that my experience is of events of over fifty years ago when I was only a small boy who did not regard such things seriously, and at this distance of time it is not easy to separate actual first hand knowledge from the contemporary hearsay. However, for what it is worth, here it is.
>
> I saw the ghost on a number of occasions, of which two are very clear in my mind. It was a harmless ghost — or at any rate it did not appear to upset or affect people and those immediately concerned took little notice of it. I remember, however, that the dogs disliked and apparently feared it.
>
> It was a tall female figure dressed in black and with a handkerchief held to her face as if crying. To the best of my knowledge 'she' was substantial and I have no impression of translucency.
>
> I believe 'she' was known in her lifetime to my godmother with whose family I lived for a time when I was a boy, but she would never speak of her. If this is so (I have no reason to doubt it) the ghost's original could not when I saw her have been long dead.
>
> She was not particular where or when she appeared. The two occasions I clearly remember were (1) in the garden in bright sunlight walking about and (2) in the drawing room when we made a ring around her by joining hands, from which she appeared merely to walk out between two people and then disappeared.
>
> I feel sure there were other occasions, but as I have said I was very small — the youngest of those with whom I was associated — and I dare say I was not

encouraged much to join in and had doubtless more important interests elsewhere. And I expect it is all on record. I cannot remember the name of the ghost lady, if I ever knew it; the people who afterward had the house for a time were named Despard . . .

—— Letter of Mr George Gooding to the SPR, November, 1944.

An interesting letter, and one which would seem to indicate that the haunting definitely preceded the Despard family's inhabiting the house, despite the paucity of direct evidence for this. If the house was known in the immediate neighbourhood to be haunted, it would certainly explain the frequent changes of name given it, and also the fact that it was offered during the summer of 1879 or 1880 at a rental of £60.00 a year — a ridiculously low figure even for those days. It is not necessarily so very surprising either if, in the event the house was known locally to be haunted, Miss Despard could get little or no information about it, even when her situation became known, and the family began to investigate the history of the premises. The landlord obviously lived in the neighbourhood, and had friends there — as witness the behaviour of General Annesley. Just as obviously, Mrs Imogen Swinhoe had lived in the neighbourhood, and may have had friends there. Certainly it is likely that her domestic circumstances were generally known, as she kept servants, as did most of the families in the immediate area, and servants talk, both to each other and to their employers. As Miss Despard managed to speak to at least one of Henry Swinhoe's children, it is probable that they too did not live far away. Mr Gooding's godmother obviously knew the identity of the agent of the apparition, and may still have been living in the district when the Despards lived there, but she would not speak of the matter even within her own family. There may have been many women locally who — for reasons of friendship, religion, concern for the living, or simple distaste — felt, as she did, that the affair should rest if it could. Effectively, we know much too little about the social environment of the place at the time to know how much local knowledge may have been discreetly concealed.

After the Despards left the house in 1893, it again remained empty for some years. In 1898 a Mr L.M. Wallich opened a preparatory school for boys there. He called the house 'Inholmes'. It would appear from a letter written to Mr B. Abdy Collins after he had published an article about the matter in *Psychic News* (and later a book: *The Cheltenham Ghost*, Psychic Press Limited, 1948), that the haunting went through a fresh cycle during the nine-year life of the school on the site:

> *In your article in this week's* Psychic News *on 'Explanation of Ghosts' you state that the Cheltenham Ghost was not seen after 1889.*
>
> *This is incorrect!*
>
> *Forty-five years ago, when I was a child, I lived within a stone's throw of this house. I had not heard its sinister reputation and was accustomed to wander at will around the quiet, shady road in which the house stands.*
>
> *One beautiful sunny morning I was irresistibly drawn towards the tall iron gate of the house, just in time to see a little old lady descend the steps of the garden door at the side of the house.*
>
> *When she saw me peering through the iron gate, she hurried towards me. I can see her now — after all these years — her dress of black to her ankles, little white lace neck trimming, and her hair covered with a white lace cap. I waited unconcernedly for her to reach me, but when about a yard away she suddenly stopped, and her hands went up to her face and she cried bitterly into a small white handkerchief.*
>
> *I felt so dreadfully sorry for her and said out loud, 'What is the matter — oh, what is the matter.' She did not answer me, but completely disappeared.*
>
> *When I told my mother of the lady who was rude enough to go away without answering me, she questioned me about her appearance and then looked horror-struck, and impressed me that I was not ever again to visit the road or house unless with a grown-up.*
>
> *Within a short time of this experience, I can well remember a great outcry about this same house. I remember a most unruly crowd surrounding the property at midnight, and the local police scattering them.*
>
> *The house remained empty and the lovely garden derelict — weeds growing right up to the entrance gate.*
>
> *Then it was turned into a Boarding School for Boys — the upper stories being turned into dormitories — but it was not long before there was the usual 'fuss'. The old lady was encountered on the stairs — in the corridors — even in the boys' dormitories — always leaving the house in broad daylight from the garden door and wandering down the short drive.*
>
> *The maids left in terror and eventually the place was*

again closed. One small boy was very ill from fright and nearly died . . .

— *Light Magazine*, Spring 1958.

As part of his research into the 'Cheltenham Ghost' for *Hauntings and Apparitions*, Andrew Mackenzie searched copies of the local papers of the time for mention of this last event, and also appealed for information about the school in the press, sadly without result.

When the school closed, the house remained empty until 1910, when it was taken by the Order of St Ursulines. The nuns stayed for two years, and in 1913 St Anne's Nursery College was opened at the premises. In 1935 the house was bought by the Diocese of Gloucester and retained by them until 1970. In 1973 it was bought by a housing association and converted into flats. Isolated reports of apparent sitings continued into the early 1920s, one witness stating, 'We used to go and see the ghost dancing across the lawn on many occasions when I was a boy. It used to be quite a common experience with the boys of the town.' By his own account Mr Abdy-Collins' correspondent saw it in the 1930s, but there have been no reported sitings at the house in recent times.

'Record of a Haunted House' is considered to be one of the best studies of an apparitional haunting, and the evidence is thought to be very good, although there has been some controversy about the identity of the apparition, mainly because its face was usually hidden by the handkerchief held to the eyes. Various suggestions have been put forward over the years in an effort to explain the events in the house during the course of the Despards' residence there, but these do not stand up to close examination. It is, to my mind in any event, a highly suspicious circumstance that the house changed hands and name so often, and stood empty for so long, even before the Despards took it and the fact of the haunting became common knowledge, and certainly the descriptions of the apparition, given by witnesses widely separated in time, are remarkably similar.

Interestingly, too, although no sitings have been reported at the house itself for many years, another very similar apparition to that seen by Rosina Despard has been seen in Cotswold Lodge, a house which once stood on the opposite side of the road from the Despards' house and which has now been demolished. That apparition was seen in 1961 by William Thorne and his son John, and was described as being that of a woman in a long black dress, whose features were not visible due to the handkerchief which was held to the face. From such a description as this, it would be very easy to identify this apparition with that seen so many years before in the house across the street, but why it should suddenly appear at Cotswold Lodge, where there was no previous report of it, is unknown.

— *Part 2* —

THEORIES

— 8 —

Theories 1: Hallucinations, Telepathy and Extra-sensory Perception

Theories on 'ghosts' can be divided into two categories: those based on *hallucinations*, *telepathy* and *extra-sensory perception*, and those which are *animistic*, that is to say based upon the premise that the soul is the vital principle of organic development and that the spirit exists separately from the body. In this chapter we shall be looking at three important theories which fall into the first category.

1. Apparitions as Mental Hallucinations.

Edmund Gurney, a founder member of the Society for Psychical Research, believed apparitions to be mental hallucinations created by individuals in response to telepathic impulse, either spontaneous or deliberate. He felt that such hallucinations were completely delusive — sensory precepts lacking any objective basis. They were projections of the percipient's brain created as a response to the instructions of the agent, by which his senses were deceived. In his view, subjective hallucinations differed from the veridical variety only as to the area of their source within the brain itself.

Apparitions of the living, experimental cases and crisis apparitions were all classed by Gurney as 'phantasms of the living'. Crisis apparitions are, as you will recall, so categorized even where the agent has been actually deceased for up to 12 hours. This apparently arbitrary time limit came to exist because crisis cases were, in Gurney's view, due to deferred telepathy. His theory was that the percipient of such apparitions subconsciously receives the message from the agent at the moment of death or before it, but that the message lies dormant or is actively suppressed for a time, usually until the percipient enters some quiet mental state that allows it to work its way through to the surface of consciousness. The percipient then suitably embodies it, projects it forth and so perceives it apparently externally as an apparition.

Post-mortem cases Gurney felt to be purely subjective, in that they occur too long after death to be attributable to deferred telepathy from the living, and do not coincide with any crisis-event which might point to their being telepathic.

The whole edifice of the theory of deferment rests primarily upon the results of experiments in the telepathic transference of taste. These established that there is, in some cases, a slight lapse of time between an agent's transmittal of an idea and a percipient's receipt of it — 12 hours being the maximum time considered reasonable to allow for deferment of receipt. Those experiments alone would not, of course, be sufficient to support the idea that apparitions perceived as a result of some crisis are deferred ideas transmitted by the agent in the last moments of life, but deferred hallucinations are also easily produced by hypnosis, if delay is part of the suggestion, and this was felt to be supportive of the theory of deferment in crisis cases.

It is, however, hard to see why delay *should* form part of the suggestive process, and it might therefore be felt that the whole categorization of crisis cases should be reassessed. But even the most cursory look at the accumulated evidence serves to show that apparitions which are adjudged to be crisis apparitions under the present system exhibit in the main behaviour quite different from that shown by apparitions which fall into other categories (post-mortem apparitions included), and thus that the crisis category is capable of standing on its own merits and without reference to the theory of deferment at all.

Reciprocal cases, which are among the most difficult to fit into any theoretical mould, Gurney considered to be the result of 'contagion', the primary recipient 'infecting' the others by telepathically transmitting that which had been in the first instance transmitted to him. He eventually extended this theory to cover collective cases as well, considering, in the first instance, three possibilities likely to cover the available facts. These possibilities were:

- that the apparition might be physically present in space where it is seen

- that an agent might telepathically influence two or more percipients independently, each of whom would then respond by creating his own sensory image
- that an agent would (as in his theory of reciprocal cases) telepathically influence a primary percipient who would then in turn act as agent and telepathically influence a secondary percipient.

The first two of these ideas he rejected out of hand, adopting finally the third explanation after modifying it by adding that individuals collected together in the same place were usually mentally occupied to a large extent with similar topics, a factor which he felt would certainly facilitate 'infection'.

2. Apparitions as Etheric Images Created by a Mental Act.

In 1888 Frederick Myers, another founder member of the Society for Psychical Research and a pioneer in the study of consciousness, put forward the theory that apparitions of the living and of the dead were telepathic phenomena. He agreed with Gurney that it was the percipient who embodied the message received in the sensory form which constituted the apparition, but was not wholly consistent about this theory, and finally came to hold quite separate ideas about one part of the evidence at least.

Like Gurney, Myers rejected the theory of physical presence, and thought the idea of independent influence (the second of Gurney's 'possibilities' referred to above) improbable. However, he also rejected the idea that hallucinations might be contagious, pointing out that subjective hallucinations appeared never to be so, as they certainly would (or should) were any category of hallucination at all 'infectious'.

Again like Gurney, Myers thought that all apparitions represented a manifestation of persistent personal energy, and that they were not, as a rule, representative of conscious intelligence, being instead automatic projections from consciousness centred elsewhere. However, he agreed with Gurney as to their causation only in the case of single percipients, considering that, in collective cases in any event, apparitions occupied space in a real way:

> . . . I hold, that when the phantasm is discerned by more than one person at once (and on some but not all other occasions) it is actually effecting a change in that portion of space where it is perceived, although not, as a

rule, in the matter which occupies that place. It is, therefore, not optically or acoustically perceived, perhaps no rays of light are reflected nor waves of air set in motion; but an unknown form of supernormal perception, not necessarily acting through sensory end-organs, comes into play.

The point at which an apparition appeared Myers called 'a phantasmogenetic centre', i.e. 'a point in space so modified by the presence of a spirit that it becomes perceptible to persons materially present near it'. He spoke elsewhere of 'actual spatial changes induced in the metetherial, but not in the material world', which would seem to imply that he believed that space interpenetrated the metetherial as well as the material plane, while matter did not.

Effectively, therefore, Myers was proposing the psychical, but not the physical, invasion of space, stating:

The concept of psychical incursion or invasion implies that some movement bearing some relation to space as we know it is accomplished; that the invading spirit modifies a certain portion of space, not materially or optically, but in such a manner that specially susceptible persons may perceive it.

In his view, when a 'projector' of consciousness, whether living or dead, viewed a distant scene as though he were standing within or in front of it, obtaining in the process correct information about it, then there could be an actual modification of space at that spot. Such a modification would not, of course, be material in the usually accepted meaning of that word, but it would nevertheless cause people — particularly 'sensitive' people — to perceive an image corresponding to the projector at the focus point of his projection. In other words, Myers considered a projector, although not physically present at the spot projected to, to be mentally and therefore in some way *spatially* present there.

It is important at this point to appreciate that while Myers rejected the idea of telepathic deferment and considered the psychical invasion of space to be in some cases not only possible but probable, he was not postulating the existence of an etheric body, or that the extrusion of such a body would result in its visibility to a suitably sensitive person positioned — either accidentally or deliberately — at the focus point. Instead there was '. . . a real transference of something from the agent, involving an alteration of some kind in a particular kind of space', and that the something was in the nature of a 'seed' from which the optical illusion of an apparition could grow in a particular spatial dimension which Myers called 'the metetherial'. This is quite a different proposition to the idea of an etheric body. If his theory were correct, it would mean that the projector's perception of himself at that moment would determine the appearance of his 'apparition', and ergo the clothing and accessories perceived would relate to that perception of self, and would not be created *ad hoc*.

Obviously, Myers' theory could be applied not only to apparitions of the living, but to post-mortem apparitions too, the only difference so far as he was concerned between those two categories being that the 'seed', once the projector had died, would be permanently detached from the body, rather than just temporarily so. The theory could also be applied to ghosts or haunting apparitions, as these could well be based on the 'dreams of the dead'.

At first glance, this would appear to be a rather startling idea, but in fact it is quite true that the behaviour of haunting ghosts closely resembles the behaviour of apparitions of the living — particularly if the living person is, as Myers termed it, 'psychorragic', i.e. breaking loose the soul from the material body, or chronically liable to an involuntary detachment of his 'seed'. Apparitions of the living often result when the projector is in a day-dream state (as was Miss Dorothy Scott in Case No. 1) and quite unconscious of the fact that he is projecting. In view of the similarity of result, there is no real reason why haunting ghosts should not come about due to a similar activity on the part of the dead, with desire of being in a particular place replaced by, perhaps, strong recollection of being there — always assuming that something of the human constitution survives physical death.

However, Myers was not quite consistent as to this aspect of his theory either, as he also postulated that, in the case of haunted houses or places, the faculty of *retrocognition* (knowledge of the past paranormally acquired) might be at the root of percipients' experiences. In his book *Human Personality* he states:

> I think that the curious question as to the influence of certain houses in generating apparitions may be included under the broader heading of retrocognition. That is to say, we are not here dealing with a special condition of certain houses, but a branch of the wide problem as to the relation of supernormal phenomena to time. Manifestations which occur in haunted houses depend, let us

say, on something which has taken place a long time ago . . .

Myers himself admitted that his theory suffered 'from the complexity and apparent absurdity inevitable in dealing with phenomena which greatly transcend known laws', but there is no doubt that it could explain the causal factors behind some apparitional phenomena very adequately, and certainly it has the merit of explaining why, in collective cases, percipients see the *same* apparition rather than just *an* apparition, which Gurney's theory does not. Myers' theory, however, also obviously implies some sort of survival of death (although quite what sort is never made really clear) — an idea which Gurney was not prepared to accept.

3. Apparitions as Psychological Hallucinations.

G.M. Tyrrell, rejecting both the theory of apparitions as physical entities and Myers' theory of the psychical invasion of space, agreed with Gurney as to the telepathic origin of hallucinations, but thought that apparitions were *psychological*, rather than mental, phenomena. He suggested that they were idea patterns produced by the subconscious of the percipient with or without the co-operative assistance of the unconscious of the person represented by the apparition. Interestingly, so far as causation was concerned, he stated that the explanation for these events should be 'sought in the processes of sense perception' rather than in telepathy pure and simple. For Tyrrell, then, apparitions were false perceptions, elaborate sensory constructs originating in the personalities of an agent and a percipient working together.

In order to explain the mechanics of this theory, Tyrrell introduced the interesting but complicated concept of the 'Stage Carpenter' and the 'Producer', each of which symbolically represented separate psychological constituents of the personality. The theatre of operation in which he thought that those constituents worked was a level of being where the spatial apartness of the physical no longer applied. Acting together, Producer and Stage Carpenter of both agent and percipient would conspire to produce an apparitional drama based upon an idea pattern which might originate in telepathic influence, hypnotism, drugs, anaesthetics, memory or imagination, complexes, hopes, fears, etc. The drama itself — or what the percipient eventually 'saw' and experienced apparently external to himself — would be produced piecemeal from previously experienced and internalized sensory input. The more complete and perfect the resulting hallucination (and Tyrrell drew up a description of what constituted the 'perfect apparition'), the more efficient the Stage Carpenter at his job.

For Tyrrell, therefore, telepathy was not the transmission of information from one mind to another — as it most certainly was for Gurney and Myers — but only a way of referring to the non-separateness which all human beings share at what he called the 'mid-level strata of personality' where, as previously mentioned, the notion of spatial apartness does not apply.

Collective and reciprocal cases he explained by applying the same principles, stating that bystanders of the primary percipient would be drawn into the apparitional drama if the underlying theme of the drama required it. In other words, the precipitating idea in the agent's mind of being in another place and visible to the percipient there would be so arranged by the Stage Carpenter and the Producer of agent and percipient alike as to make the resulting apparition visible to bystanders if bystanders happened to be there. Indeed, if bystanders did happen to be present, the resulting apparitional production would be aided by their individual Stage Carpenters and Producers as well and would become a co-operative production by the distant agent, the percipient, and any person accompanying the percipient at the time.

Despite Tyrrell's emphasis on apparitions as psychological phenomena, however, he did not wholly discard the idea that a deceased person might, in some instances, be the agent necessary for the production of the phenomena, if only because it was, in his own words '. . . hard to find a plausible candidate for the agency other than a deceased person'. A rather grudging admission of the possibility of survival of death of some kind and, again, the idea of survival is not really explored.

These three theories are not, of course, the only current ones of this kind, but they are the most important and form the basis for many of the more recently developed theories of the same nature. All three theories agree on some points, and it will become obvious that each of them agrees to some extent with some aspects of the theories held by animists too.

— *9* —

Theories 2: Animism and Survival

Two main ideas fall into this category. The first is that developed by spiritualists, the second that favoured by occultists. Both of these theories have points in common with those contained in the last chapter, but they cannot be described with similar ease because they are in fact not theories at all, but tenets, dogma, parts of established belief systems from which they cannot be isolated without becoming incomprehensible. The main outline of those systems must, therefore, be briefly delineated here so that the tenets/theories themselves may be understood.

1. Spiritualism — Apparitions as Spirits of the Departed.

It is important to understand from the outset that the *raison d'être* of spiritualism is to prove survival of death and the reality and practicality of communication between the living and the dead. Spiritualists believe that death in the physical world equates with birth into a subtler level of being. Experiences at that level are not identical in every case, simply because no two human beings are alike. Also, although most communicators who trouble to mention it insist upon the painless nature of dying, the manner of death itself may influence the nature of the experiences which take place directly after it, as may the attitude of the individual. Thus those people who expect to experience a life after death are considered to adjust more quickly to their new environment than those who do not and, where death occurs unexpectedly or very quickly, the deceased may persist in the illusion of physical life and so become confused — a condition that is less likely to occur where death is preceded by a long illness.

Telepathic rapport between the deceased and loved ones is considered by spiritualists to be common in the period immediately following death, although less easy to sustain as time goes on. Such a rapport can be initiated by the living or the dead, and where it is initiated by the living, it can supposedly delay the beginning of an active discarnate life on the part of the deceased (as, indeed, can excessive or prolonged grief, which is upsetting to the departed soul, and constantly recalls it to the side of the bereaved).

The subtle world to which the deceased is transported upon death is primarily a mental one, where everything is moulded by thought. Thus the nature of the thoughts of the departed is considered to mould his immediate experience, because his environment is mentally created by himself. This is believed to be why the majority of the recently dead describe their new surroundings as being a pleasant sunlit landscape, full of features and people familiar and dear to them. This landscape, which spiritualists have called the *Summerlands*, reflects the thoughts and inner condition of the deceased. It looks perfectly solid and earth-like, but it is simply a completely illusory mental construct. The other side of the attractive coin represented by the Summerlands is the *Winterland*, a condition that is also completely illusory, and which is created, it is believed, by selfishness and self-imposed isolation.

The deceased's residence in the Summer (or Winter) lands is not intended to endure indefinitely, although no pressure is placed upon him to leave if he does not wish to do so. The Summer and Winterlands are places, or rather states of being, which exist only to provide a resting-place for the soul, a chance for the deceased to acclimatize to his new condition, to discover and realize the importance of the inner self and consciousness, and to learn early lessons in the use to which the creative power of the mind and emotions might be put. Eventually, however, the deceased should progress by his own will to what is called the *Judgement*, a very important event which will take up a considerable length of his time and exercise decisive effects on his future.

This Judgement is not considered to be a final event, the outcome of which will determine the soul's dispatch to a 'heaven' or a 'hell'. Rather, it is believed to be a self-judgement, a sort of stock-taking of positive and negative qualities and acts which will reveal lessons to be learned and highlight qualities which might be improved. The deceased must, to be sure, come to terms with himself, identify areas in which he must improve, recognize his mistakes, and pay for them in self-realization, but this is a minor purgatory hardly worth the name, and one in which the soul receives help from spiritual teachers, rather than a sentence to eternal damnation. Once it is satisfactorily over, the soul can continue on, through the *First*, *Second* and *Third Heavens*.

The purpose of the First Heaven is to intensify perception, deepen emotional relationships, allow the deceased to live again through the credit and debit sides of his former life, and commence the discovery of his real, whole, being. It is effectively the soul's first step toward shedding the personality it developed in its most recent life, and so is in reality the approach to what is called the *Second Death*.

The Second Death stands between the First and Second Heavens, and it involves the laying aside of the personality. Because of this, it can prove to be a serious stumbling block to the soul's progress, and lead to much time being spent in the First Heaven. Fearing to discard the only self it ever remembers having known, the soul may for some time hesitate to do so, and will in the process impede its own access to its real self, its true individuality. The Second Death, however, must be undergone, as it is considered to be precursive to entry into the Second Heaven, where consciousness must be transferred from the transitory *personality* to the more enduring *individuality*.

In the Second Heaven, having achieved access to himself, the deceased will come to realize how far his personality in his last life deviated from the individuality of which it was supposed to be an image and, because he will also have access to memories of his former lives and personalities, he will be able to see clearly the pattern of purpose and meaning to be traced there, and how far he has fallen short of fulfilling either pattern or meaning. With these new facts at hand, he will commence to construct a blueprint of the new life he must undergo on earth, which will follow a course harmonious with his causal self, and will be designed both to forward his progress and to correct the deviations created by his most recent and former lives. He will, too, discover the group to which he belongs, and come to realize its destiny and purpose and his place within it. Much time will therefore be spent in re-establishing links with other members of that group.

Prior to entry into the Second Heaven, the deceased will have retained that form which he took in his most recent life, although if he grew old in that life this will 'regress' to the condition in which it looked and felt best — usually, but not always, towards youth. In the Second Heaven, however, the deceased will experience a change of his outer form. It will become less distinctly human, and more like an energy pattern. Despite the fact that the deceased will at this point commence living increasingly as part of a Group Soul, the energy pattern will be completely individual and recognizable to others existing at a similar level.

The deceased will enter then the Third Heaven, a place of archetypal ideas and inspirations, prior and preparatory to reincarnating into a new body or dispensing with reincarnation altogether. This latter choice is not automatically open to all, but when the soul has been perfected and the debt to earth paid, then it may either choose to reincarnate again with some specific and important purpose in mind, or to travel away from reincarnation and towards the Divine Principle. This involves the shedding of the individuality — it sinks into the consciousness of the Divine as the personality sank into the individuality at the Second Death — and is the ultimate goal of all. Where this choice is not offered, however, the soul must spend its time in the Third Heaven implanting deep within its consciousness as much as it can of its image of its future self. When circumstances permit, it will then commence to reincarnate and begin the whole cycle again.

But what of apparitions? So far as spiritualists are concerned, these may be:

- in the case of what has been referred to as crisis apparitions, the spirits of the departed returning to assure loved ones of the fallacy of death and the reality of continuing being
- in the case of post-mortem apparitions, either the former or confused persons who have failed, or refuse, to realize the fact of their own death
- in the case of hauntings, the spirits of the departed trapped in matter by desire, confusion or the idea or fact of guilt.

Communication with the dead is conducted through the channel of *mediums* (individuals who have the facility to carry on such communication) and it is upon the 'evidence' provided via mediumship that spiritualists base their belief in survival of death. Mediumship may be physical or mental, but the greater proportion of the 'evidence' for this survival comes through mental mediumship, and this can take many forms. The medium may be entranced, for example, or in a slightly disassociated state. If he is entranced, then his personality will be completely dispossessed by the entity with whom he has established a channel. The entity will speak directly through him, utilizing his vocal cords. This is the most advanced form of mediumship. If the medium is simply in a disassociated state, then he may (a) 'see' or 'hear' the entity with whom he has established a channel, and so be able to transmit messages from that entity to the living, or (b) see symbolic visions which he must learn to interpret before relaying the message encoded into them. Simpler forms of mediumship include working with planchette or ouija board, or developing automatic writing. As far as this is concerned, the state of mind of the medium during the production of automatic writing may be anything from normal wakefulness to deep trance.

2. Apparitions as Astral or Etheric Bodies.

The belief system adopted by occultists has much in common with that embraced by spiritualists, but its main thrust and its vocabulary are very different. Spiritualists wish to prove survival of death not just to a few people but to the population at large, so as to alleviate grief and encourage the prudent adoption of good principles in the living. This they hope to achieve via their churches, their platform work, their healing services and the example of their own lives. The purpose of the occultist is to prove survival of death for *himself*, to encourage his *own* good principles, and to progress through the Second Death without the necessity of first deceasing, thus obtaining access to his individuality and his group, the knowledge of his previous lives, his true self, and his true purpose while still alive. His motto is 'Know Thyself', and through the medium of his training and the exercises he must complete every day, which effectively constitute a painful course of unceasing self-analysis, he must learn to control his thoughts (which he believes to be formative on every level), know himself, and master the means whereby consciousness and emotion may be used creatively. Proselyting in any form is forbidden him: his absolute secrecy is essential and is often demanded under oath. He may not speak or in any way publish anything given, shown, or explained to him without the permission of those he has accepted as his superiors — and that permission is not often forthcoming.

At first glance, and contrasted with the more obviously humanitarian aims of the spiritualist, this may seem to be a selfish course, but in fact it is not. The closer the personality comes to the individuality (which is, after all, its archetypal reality), the nearer the purpose of the life to that blueprint constructed in what has been called above the 'Second Heaven', the faster the soul will progress. The faster the soul progresses, the faster the group progresses, and the faster the group progresses, the faster humanity progresses. As humanity, or so it is believed, is responsible, as the biblical 'Lord of the Earth', for both the planetary body and the 'lesser brethren' (by which is meant animals and so on), the faster it progresses, the faster they, too, progress along the evolutionary spiral that leads to eventual perfection and absorption into the Divine Principle whence all came.

Despite the similarity of belief — and, in the end, purpose — between spiritualists and occultists, on the subject of apparitions the two groups seriously part company for, so far as occultists are concerned, apparitions are not departed spirits but etheric or astral images, created by a mental act and thus imprinted upon the 'photographic plate' of the all-pervasive *ether*. At the root of this theory is the idea that all is Mind, and that the difference between the physical, the etheric and the yet higher and more subtle levels of being is therefore simply a matter of degree. To the occultist, literally everything is living, and all living things possess a series of bodies of varying subtlety. That on the etheric level is a perfect facsimile of the physical body, and in fact determines its shape, but the etheric shape is in turn determined by factors inherent in bodies or states yet more subtle. Thus, at the highest level, the chair which is a physical object in the material world is simply an expression of the will to sit, and that which is a human being at the material level is simply an expression of the will to be — 'will' in this context being the will of the Creator, of which all things are an expression.

All the various 'bodies' which manifest as material beings or things of any kind are considered to exist simultaneously, but in different kinds of space. Only one of them (the physical body) is really subject to linear time, as time, too, is thought to become more subtle as it 'ascends' the levels of being, until it finally becomes an Eternal Now, a sort of block in which all events exist simultaneously.

The *etheric body*, which is thought to be electrical in nature, is attached to the physical body during life, but may be detached from it either spontaneously or deliberately. It is this body that is thought to be the vehicle of consciousness for apparitions of the living, crisis apparitions, and out-of-body experiences. The etheric body, however, is believed to be destroyed shortly after death, dissipating as the physical body decays or is otherwise disposed of, at which time consciousness moves into a yet subtler vehicle. This new vehicle is an *astral body*, and it is this body that is considered by occultists to be that which 'appears' in post-mortem cases, and in some, but not all, cases of haunting apparitions.

It is important to realize that, according to occult theory, the *astral light* — a substance which corresponds in some respects with Myers' 'metetherial' — is a plastic substance somewhere between mind and matter that interpenetrates the physical and is capable of being moulded by thought. Two points must therefore be borne in mind so far as occult theory is concerned. The first is that it is possible — either deliberately or accidentally — to both build and inhabit an astral body that is not part of one's own personal series of bodies and that may or may not resemble the physical self at all, dependent upon the image that is in the mind of the builder. Such a 'body of light', built deliberately, may be used as a vehicle of consciousness by its 'owner' and despatched anywhere in space and time. Clothing and accessories under these circumstances are created *ad hoc*. The same 'body of light', however, formulated accidentally and as a result of strong emotion, is more likely to take the shape of an animal of some kind and, being spontaneous, is not under the control of the 'owner's' conscious mind at all, although it may, by an effort of will, be brought under such control.

Secondly, the malleability of the ether under the impact of the human mind, and particularly of the human mind under the stress of strong emotion, means that 'pictures' are implanted in it at the point where those emotions were originally conceived, and that 'tracks' are formed in space by that means. To occultists, therefore, some hauntings are simply 'pictures' in the ether that will run again and again until they finally wear out, just as a regular film would eventually wear out under the strain of constant use. If the 'picture' relates to the individual who forms it, then it will be his image that is recorded, together with its associated emotions. If the 'picture', however, is formed by fear or mental stress, then the image will be that of an archetypal figure that is fearsome to its creator, and will appear so to those who behold it thereafter. Occultists consider that such 'tracks in space' are likely to be more easily formed, and to endure longer, where environmental conditions are favourable — in wetlands, for instance, or near buildings constructed of porous stone like granite — and that they are perceptible to 'sensitive' persons because they have spatial presence and validity.

While both occultists and spiritualists therefore reject the idea of physical presence, occultists accept the possibility of telepathic exchanges between the living and the dead, but do not believe that these of themselves result in the production of apparitional phenomena, although they may form part of the experience, usually taking the place of speech. Neither do occultists accept the ideas of telepathic influence or projection or contagion, save in certain experimental cases involving comparatively large groups of people — where Tyrrell's theory as to the nature of the phenomenon, and its psychological origin and mode of production is accepted absolutely — or where the deliberately constructed 'body of light' forms the vehicle of consciousness. Other experimental cases, apparitions of the living and crisis apparitions are considered to be etheric extrusions as per Myers' 'seed' theory (save that Myers was not postulating the existence of such a body), while postmortem apparitions are considered to be manifestations of the astral body, as are 'active' hauntings, that is, hauntings where the apparition is responsive to the percipient. Hauntings where the apparition is non-responsive are thought to be 'tracks in space', and thus while occultists agree with Myers that retrocognition may on some occasions be the faculty that allows percipients to experience a haunting, they disagree as to whether a house or place may by its environmental positioning or structure create a 'special condition' which could encourage the formation of a haunting in the first instance.

In *all* cases apparitions are considered by occultists to be spatially present, as Myers considered *some* apparitions to be, but in no case is an apparition considered to be the spirit of a deceased person. It is a portion of consciousness, and not the soul or spirit, which, it is thought, must reside upon the plane or level proper to its state at the time, either the material level or the First, Second or Third Heavens. In crisis, post-mortem, and 'active' hauntings, the apparition is indeed felt to be indicative of proof of survival, but only in living, experimental and crisis cases and those of active haunting (which are considered to be 'aberrant' in any event in light of the fact that such a haunting is thought to be the result of an abnormal and retarding mental condition on the part of the haunter) is the mind and personality of the haunting being thought to be present to any large degree, and the spirit to any degree at all.

Like spiritualists, occultists use mediumship (which they have termed 'mediatorship'), but again they use it rather differently. Every practising occultist must develop a channel between his personality and his individuality, so as to assist the eventual merger of these two parts of the self. This is an accepted form of mediatorship developed by occultists by way of meditation, but much the same effect results in some cases where other methods are used. In his book *Mediumship and*

Survival (Heinemann, 1982), Alan Gauld describes the appearance of what he has called 'quasi-personalities' through the practice of spiritualist mediumship, which may display opinions, talents, literacy levels, and even intelligence, different to and far greater than that of the medium. Such personalities are recognized by occultists as manifestations of individuality, but because they are capable of, say, writing music, speaking or reading in languages unknown to the medium, or dictating long cosmological treatises, they can be easily mistaken for deceased personalities — which, of course, they are not.

Having developed a channel between his personality and individuality, the occultist will then go on to try to communicate, not, as the spiritualist primarily does, with deceased persons based in the First Heaven, but with what he terms 'contacts', spiritual teachers who will show him the best way to develop himself through his work.

Both occultists and spiritualists believe that psychic faculties are natural to human beings, present to a greater or lesser extent in everyone, that mediumship is to some degree hereditary, and that both 'psychism' and mediumship are capable of being further developed by exercise and practice. They believe, too, that 'natural' or undeveloped mediumship abounds in the population at large, and that a medium, whether developed or not, may — depending upon whether he is 'positively' or 'negatively' sensitive — actually assist in the production of psychic phenomena, consciously or unconsciously. Thus, for animists, too, perception itself is not always a passive act, for it depends in some instances not only upon the percipient being in the right frame of mind, but also upon his having the capability of active participation in a paranormal event. This is not to say, however, that the theories set forth in the previous chapter are accepted by animists, or that 'positive' sensitives are thought to assist phenomena by embodying a message received telepathically in a sensory form then projecting it outwards from themselves. For animists, participation in any apparitional drama begins and ends with the provision of an energy originating in the subtle, rather than the material, body of the individual concerned.

— *10* —

Reconciliation and Conclusions

Theories are essential to progress and understanding and are therefore excellent and useful things; unfortunately they are also extremely dangerous. Implicit in every theory is the demand that one should either agree with it wholeheartedly or reject it entire. Where several conflicting theories exist then the implication is that one should instantly assume the mantle of an arbitrator and make a choice. Once such a decision has been made, it is only too easy to distort fact so that the chosen idea bears the appearance of being faultless. Obviously, this is not good enough, and leads nowhere, but it nevertheless all too often occurs simply because it constitutes the line of least resistance and demands less personal effort. Of course, in a perfect world theories would conflict less violently and less often, be more readily comprehensible, more obviously capable of reconciliation, and so cause less contention — but our world, alas, is not perfect. Thus we are consistently presented with the difficulty of discovering which, of many possible truths, is actually *the* truth, and of restraining ourselves from falling in love with an idea and then marrying it, for better or worse.

An even-handed discussion of current theories on apparitional phenomena is in any event rendered difficult by the nature of animistic theories, which have an irresistible appeal for most us — at least on an emotional level — for obvious reasons, and thus represent a major stumbling block to level-headed communication. Never mind that survival of death is not really the issue at hand. As the theories stand, it cannot help but appear that what is being offered is either the sure and certain hope of continuing existence on the one hand, or a series of paradoxical ifs, buts, and maybes on the other. In such a contest, where the choice is apparently between the assurance of eternal life or the possibility of a brief span of light followed by perpetual darkness, science is in a no-win situation. It is a rare person who can with equanimity contemplate the idea of eventual total dissolution, the concept of personal non-being, and the tendency is therefore to vigorously reject any theory which tends to prove that that might well be the eventual fate of us all.

Debate is further complicated by the complexity of scientific theories, which demand so much effort of understanding and yet still fail to present that satisfying appearance of rounded wholeness, that 'yes, we have an answer for everything' that is the hallmark of their animistic counterparts. Science, too, uses words and phrases that are unsympathetic and psychologically cold, and produces concepts that stretch credulity to the limit simply because they postulate human mental abilities so powerful as to be — to say the least — very attractive, but rather improbable. It is consequently very important when evaluating the theories set out in the previous chapters to understand that (a) science is not anti-survival, (b) a belief in survival does not free the believer from postulating telepathy, ESP (extra-sensory perception), or even hallucinations, (c) animistic and scientific theories have a great deal in common, and (d) plumping for science in a spirit of defiance will not prevent your having to believe at least six impossible things before breakfast!

Where many theories exist as to a single subject and yet are based upon the same data — as those relating to apparitions are — then likenesses between them are certain to exist despite conflicting interpretations of fact. If those likenesses are matched one with the other, and the whole tested against fact, then it is possible not only to see where individual theories fail, but also to produce a new, compound, theory that reflects all the best qualities of the old ones. Such a theory will not, of course, be the theory to end all theories, as new data could overturn it at any moment, but it is probable that it will cover most eventualities, contain at least a modicum of truth, and so be less likely to end in the blind alley of failure of function.

In order, therefore, to see where likenesses between theories exist and to test the whole against what we know to be factual, it is necessary to recapitulate what we know to be true of apparitions. Then it will be possible to see where the theories agree with those truths (and with each other) and where they do not. Fact, so far as apparitions are concerned, is what has been seen and observed, felt and experienced in a majority of cases.

You will recall that we commenced with five theories, which can be briefly summarized as follows:

1. Gurney: Apparitions as mental hallucinations, created by individual percipients in response to telepathic impulses directly or indirectly received from the agent.
2. Myers: Apparitions as etheric images created currently, or in the past, by some mental act.
3. Tyrrell: Apparitions as idea patterns produced currently or recently by the subconscious levels of the percipient, with or without the co-operative assistance of the agent.
4. Spiritualists: Apparitions as spirits of the departed.
5. Occultists: Apparitions as etheric or astral images or 'tracks in space'.

In the following table, which lists all that we know about apparitions from the recorded evidence at hand, these theories are indicated by number at the right-hand side of the page. Where a particular theory agrees with the facts, a dot appears in the appropriate column.

From this chart, it is possible firstly to make the following further statements about apparitions:

Apparitions are semi-substantial in that:

1. They are described as solid and real, and visible details are described as vivid.
2. They are often perceived tactually and audibly as well as visibly, all three kinds of perception being consistent with each other.
3. They are recognizably similar to and sometimes identical with material bodies or objects.
4. Their observed details may be unknown to any living person and yet prove verifiably correct.
5. They make adjustments to physical surroundings and to people just as corporeal people would.
6. They are often seen collectively by two or more people simultaneously.

They are only semi substantial in that:

1. Their visibility is erratic. They are likely to appear and disappear suddenly, to be invisible to people who would be likely to see them if they were physically embodied, to fade in and out, and to be self-luminous.
2. They may pass through solid walls or locked doors.
3. They may rise into the air without physical support, and glide instead of walk.

Fact Number	Theory Number				
	1	2	3	4	5
1. Apparitions of the living, the dying and the dead are experienced so often and with such similarity of basic characteristics that they cannot be wholly subjective, and therefore must be accepted as part of the reality of our existence.	•	•	•	•	•
2. Apparitions are usually perceived wearing ordinary clothing and with ordinary accessories — objects they carry in their hands, for instance, or vehicles in which they ride or drive. Sometimes they are accompanied by companions, people, dogs or other animals. Accessories, companions and all will disappear when the apparition disappears.	•	•	•	•	•
3. Apparitions are often indistinguishable from living people, but at the same time are able to do things that living people cannot do — appear and disappear instantly, for example, or pass through solid matter or be independent of gravitation — and they are not therefore subject to the natural laws of the manifest world.	•	•	•	•	•
4. Apparitions usually confine their words, gestures, and activities to one idea or to a group of simple ideas, and in this respect they are not like living people, whose behaviour is more complex.	•	•	•		•
5. The appearances of apparitions tend to coincide in time with crises undergone by their agents. They often convey information about those crises to percipients.	•	•	•	•	•

Fact Number	Theory Number				
	1	2	3	4	5
6. They sometimes appear to be pre-cognitive or retrocognitive, therefore they are not subject to linear time as living people are.	•	•	•	•	•
7. They may be perceived by more than one person at once, and those people may be strangers to them or at least persons other than the person most directly emotionally involved with them.	•	•	•	•	•
8. When they are perceived collectively, then they are seen by the percipients to obey the laws of perspective so that angles of vision, interception of other objects, and changes in relative size are experienced by percipients exactly as they would be if the apparition were a living person.	•	•		•	•
9. Apparitions of the dead are seen repeatedly, even by strangers, in locations in which they were associated in life, and are likely to go through some relatively simple routine related to their life in that place whenever they are perceived.		•		•	•
10. Their characteristics may not correspond to ideas in the conscious or unconscious mind of either agent or percipient. For example, the back view of an apparition is as convincing as its front views and evidential details are often conveyed which may not have been in the mind of the agent or the percipient.				•	•
11. In experimental cases, the agent may see his own body from the outside, may be aware of being in a projected body, and may at the same time be seen elsewhere as an apparition.					•

Fact Number	Theory Number				
	1	2	3	4	5
12. Again in experimental cases, the apparitional body is used as a viewpoint for observation.					•
13. The agents of apparitions of the living may not be aware of their projection, and their attention may be actively concentrated elsewhere at the time of their projection.					•
14. A person may perceive his own apparition, which will appear to be acting normally.					•

4. They may communicate ideas without words, gestures or other symbols, i.e. telepathically.

Secondly, it is possible to clearly see that none of the theories, either scientific or animistic, can be swallowed whole as they stand, because they have too many imperfections, fail to explain all the facts, and raise too many questions to which they cannot render an adequate reply. In addition, it becomes obvious that it is experimental cases in particular that throw a spanner in the works.

The scientific theories have a pleasant, polished, and very satisfactory, unsuperstitious and down-to-earth appearance. Unfortunately, although they do cover some cases very well indeed, they fail to function adequately in others. Primarily, this is because the theorists are reluctant to admit in any category of case, whether collectively perceived or not, that some thing or being external to the percipient(s) might be objectively present, preferring to postulate instead that percipients of veridical hallucinations, having obtained information by telepathy, then proceed (for obscure psychological reasons that are never really satisfactorily explained) to convert that information into an hallucination. Further, while some of the theories allow the possibility that the information itself might have been conveyed by a deceased person, others will not countenance even that, and in all cases they demand extraordinary feats of the human mind, the real extent of which frequently pass unnoticed until they are actually spelled out.

All of the scientific theories demand ESP of a very high order on the part of persons who have not displayed any signs of this talent in the past, and who may thereafter live out their entire lives without ever doing so again. Moreover, they quite fail (a) to explain why ESP should manifest itself on a single occasion and in that specific and quite singular manner, (b) to take into account the very complex mechanics of such an act, and (c) frequently fail to fit all the available facts.

Taking the last of these points first: some post-mortem apparitions not only convey information unknown (or at least not consciously known) to the percipient, but also act in a manner absolutely characteristic of the agent in life, and display purpose, seeming to be intent upon pursuing some goal of importance to themselves and possibly the percipient, too. These factors put a considerable strain on theories dependent upon ESP, because they suggest that the experiences were imposed upon the percipients by some outside agency for a specific purpose — and that the agent, having survived bodily death, retained some interest in the living and the affairs of the living.

It is hard, too, given some of the evidence, to resist the conclusion that place, or environment, plays a decisive role in generating the phenomena. In many cases (Borley Rectory is perhaps the most famous), property which has a haunting apparition also suffers other kinds of haunting phenomena, some of which are quite objective and physical. As both haunting apparitions and haunting phenomena are relatively rare, the fact that they so frequently occur together in the same place cannot be put down to coincidence, and suggests that what causes the one also causes the other. It is hard in such cases to set either down as hallucinatory, and equally difficult to fit them into the ESP mould.

As for what hallucinatory theories demand from the average percipient (who is, after all, only the ordinary man in the street) in the first place, all save wholly subjective apparitions obey the laws of perspective and appear as three-dimensional objects. This is usually taken for granted, but what most people fail to appreciate is what this must mean to the mental engineers who are supposed to have produced the phenomena in the first place.

It has been adequately proven that (a) it demands an effort of will to project an apparition of the living, (b) the act of projection causes changes in the consciousness of the projector together with side-effects like paralysis in his living body, and (c) percipients of apparitions are often in an altered or ideal state before they experience their hallucination.

What we have not seen, and what has never been adequately proved, is that that same effort of will or change in consciousness automatically equals an act of highly-complex image creation. Whence comes the very detailed information required to construct a three-dimensional figure that obeys the laws of perspective? Certainly subjects under hypnosis are capable of creating quite complex hallucinations for themselves, but these are completely subjective and not visible to other people — as apparitions quite frequently are. Does the altered and ideal state that is manifestly a prerequisite of paranormal experience qualify as a sort of hypnotic trance, and is the telepathic command of the agent in any way like the technique and command of the hypnotist? It might be that the knowledge essential to the construction of a perfectly functioning and three-dimensional apparition exists at some deep level of consciousness, and the facts of hypnosis do tend to make it at least appear to be possible, but there is no definite proof that it is possible, and — alas — there is proof that attempts at such construction, both conscious and unconscious, are not very successful.

Occultists report experiencing great difficulty in constructing the vehicle of consciousness they call 'the body of light', even though they enjoy extensive training in visualization and learn to induce altered states of consciousness at will. Consciously produced 'bodies of light' are usually functional, but rather vague, figures in flowing robes, and bear a marked resemblance to those apparitions which are recognized as being unconsciously produced, and wholly subjective. Neither bodies of light nor subjective apparitions (nor, indeed, the subjective hallucinations of the mentally ill), however, have the complexity, the completeness, or the mental impact of their vivid, veridical brethren.

When it comes to collective perception, the problem is compounded. Every category of apparition has produced cases involving collective perception. Such apparitions appear in proper perspective to all who perceive them, obviously have dimension (they are seen full face on by the person confronting them, in back view by the person behind, left side visible to the person on the left, and so on, the whole correctly foreshortened by distance) and, moreover, are objective in that more than one person sees them simultaneously. Nevertheless, many theorists will not admit that apparitions are objectively present even in these circumstances, but persist in postulating that they are wholly subjective productions, either of the mind of the percipient alone, or the minds of the agent and the percipient working in concert. Were this to be true, it would effectively mean that not only would the percipients (and/or the percipients and the agent) have to produce the apparition in the first place, but also that they would have to continually adjust it for dimension and perspective while keeping its main details constant for the entire duration of the experience — a very tall order indeed.

The difficulty for the hallucinatory theorists here is that percipients in collective experiences usually describe the same apparition, and describe it similarly. It may be that this occurs because the apparition is produced of a common telepathic theme by persons sharing both proximity and interest, but this argument is unconvincing because, even given a common theme and the utmost precision of instruction, different people will produce different interpretations of it. Experiments in telepathy have proved that even simple ideas deliberately transmitted to several people are neither identically received nor transcribed, even though basic shapes remain constant. Thus, although all interpretations of telepathically-transmitted ideas may have likeness, they do not exhibit such similarity of design as, say, the descriptions given by the witnesses in the Despard case. To be fair, the same criteria cannot be said to apply in the Scott case, where the common theme of the clergyman was described by the various percipients in such a way that the apparition seemed to have an entire wardrobe of clerical garments — but that case was unusual in that particular. In the majority of cases of collective perception, percipients describe the same figure dressed in the same garments with the same facial expression and carrying out the same series of actions, and this cannot help but raise the question of how this similarity of description is achieved.

The major flaw in all three scientific theories, though, remains the indisputable fact of experimental cases. Gurney's theory fails to explain collective percipience or post-mortem apparitions, and Tyrrell's explanation as to the mechanics behind collective percipience seems strained and artificial. Neither takes account of experimental cases. Myers' theory depends on special etheric image creation in all cases, and this does not really work where experimental cases are concerned either. According to one study, conscious projections of living persons are essentially indistinguishable from apparitions of the dying and the dead in some 23 particulars. If conscious apparitions of the living are truly vehicles of consciousness — as they would seem from the evidence to be — then the fundamental basis of theories dependent upon ESP would be seriously undermined, because the existence of some kind of etheric counterpart to the physical body would have to be postulated.

Such an hypothesis would have far-reaching consequences. The projection of a conscious apparition involves the projected personality of the living person, and the experimenter returns to his body with full memory of his actions and observations. The behaviour of such apparitions is closely related to aspects of the conscious personality: purpose, memory, emotional attachment, feelings of guilt. If it were true that the personality and memory depended upon the continuing existence of the physical brain, then it should be possible to prove that this behaviour alters sharply once death has occurred. However, there is no evidence of such an alteration. The behaviour of apparitions of the dying and the dead differs from that of the living only in those alterations of purpose that would naturally occur upon death. This being so, it could be argued that, in some cases at least, apparitions offer proof of survival of death.

It is perhaps surprising therefore that spiritualism, the source of the most adamantly animist theory of all, figures so poorly on our chart, and interesting that it, too, founders on the rock represented by experimental cases.

It is inevitable that spiritualism, which exists to prove survival of death, should emphasize the idea that apparitions are the surviving spirits of the dead, and this may in some cases be true, but the accumulated evidence proves that it cannot be so in all cases. The fact of death, as we have seen, does not alter the basic behaviour of apparitions: consequently if all apparitions were the surviving spirits of the departed, then the markedly limited character of apparitional conversations and actions that has been observed in so many cases would not exist in any case at all. Spiritualism, however, does not base its belief in survival of death upon the existence of apparitions, or the evidence provided by their behaviour.

The spiritualist theory of survival demands far less by way of mental gymnastics on the part of the average person than do scientific theories relating to apparitions, but it demands far more of specific people, because it stands four-square on the evidence provided by mediumship. However, and setting aside absolutely the admittedly many instances where mediumship has been proved to be blatantly fraudulent, how good is that evidence? How possible is it that a medium might obtain apparently evidential information by other means? How much of what is accepted as evidence can be put down to coincidence? Most importantly, what is being postulated by way of hidden mental powers on the part of the medium?

Much depends upon the true nature of trance, and its effects upon human beings. Medical testing has proved not only that trance is quite real, but also that it is sometimes cataleptic, so that the medium would be completely unconscious of what was going on around him. Could a medium 'fish' for information from his sitters, ask them leading questions in order to obtain clues about them and their circumstances, while entranced to such a degree? Could he follow up a coincidental 'hit' whilst in such an altered state? Could he obtain information by way of ESP or telepathy while in that condition?

So far as coincidence is concerned, it must in all fairness be said that much of the information tendered by mediums is extremely banal, consisting of 'messages', the contents of which could be applicable to a wide variety of people. These messages naturally appear evidential to the people most directly concerned, because those people are actively hoping to receive such a message and are therefore predisposed to believe in it and its intimate relation to themselves when it arrives. In fact such messages are not evidential at all, because the medium could have achieved a similar effect by an admixture of chance and skill. However, *much* information is not *all* information, and where messages are not banal but, on the contrary, quite specific and precise — as some of them are — then coincidence must obviously be ruled out.

Much the same can be said of the practice of 'fishing' for information by asking leading questions of the sitter, for the possibility of deliberate 'fishing' has been precluded in some cases by the setting of strict controls. Where sitters have been instructed to make only deliberately non-committal answers to the medium's questions, and facts only obtainable by extra-sensory means still continue to be produced, then 'fishing', too, must be ruled out as a potential source of information.

Unfortunately, however, even where these two factors can be satisfactorily disposed of, absolute proof of survival remains hard to come by. Extra-sensory perception has been observed in hypnotic trance, where information has sometimes been produced which could only have been clairvoyantly or telepathically derived. Hypnosis is a method of bringing up the contents of the conscious mind or inducing a state of disassociation from the normal mind. It is essentially a process of self-suggestion, and sometimes reveals the presence of secondary or even multiple personalities in the subject. These factors raise many questions about mediumistic trance and the validity of information derived from that source so far as evidence of survival of death is concerned. What is the relationship, for example, between mediumistic and hypnotic trance? How far is the disassociation common to both conditions essential to

releasing powers of extra-sensory perception, thus allowing
the mind to gather or receive information not normally accessible to it? And are mediumistic 'controls', which purport to
be deceased human beings, simply 'split offs' of the medium's
own personality, similar to the secondary or multiple personalities sometimes revealed by hypnosis?

Where the question of 'split offs' is concerned, a very obvious
difference between the multiple personalities sometimes
revealed in hypnosis and the control personalities exhibited by
mediums in trance is that multiple personalities usually
oppose one another and the primary personality, while personalities manifesting in mediumistic trance work harmoniously
with the normal conscious aims of the medium. Trance
personalities do indeed work like well-adjusted secondary or
multiple personalities, but it cannot be proved that this is
what they are. This is particularly the case where one of those
personalities claims to be a relative or friend of the sitter, and
exhibits personality traits, opinions, quirks and so forth recognizable to the sitter as being natural to the deceased, but which
are quite alien to the medium's everyday persona and normal
conscious aims.

The factors mentioned above have all been accepted as being
'evidential' so far as survival of death is concerned, but the
question still remains: is the medium producing this apparently evidential information from data provided by the living
or the dead? Entranced mediums respond and produce information in a way very like that common in hypnotized subjects,
and may respond as readily to false suggestion. There are
examples of one living person obtaining information telepathically from another in a way closely resembling that by which
a medium claims to receive information from the dead, and it
has been proved, too, that it is quite possible to telepathically
extract facts once known to an individual but which were not
in his conscious mind at the time of the experiment. How
much, therefore, is the medium drawing on the sitter for
information? And is the medium, in some cases at least, not
representing a deceased personality at all, but simply plunder-
ing the contents of the sitter's mind? Facts given during
séances — even facts not consciously known to the sitter —
cannot therefore be accepted as proof of survival, because the
possibility of these being extracted by telepathy from the
living sitter (or from some other living source) cannot be
excluded.

But how far should this process be continued to explain
some of the information produced by mediums in trance, and
how far is too far? The theory that information obtained by

mediums is extracted by way of telepathy with the living has been extended not only to include the possibility that the contents of the minds of living persons other than the sitter may be accessible to him, but also that anything ever thought or known might be accessible. Are these suggestions reasonable, and what is the proposed mechanism involved?

If a medium obtains information from a sitter, or a living person not present at the sitting and not known to him, or from some universal data-bank, how does he do it? Can he do it alone or only in concert with the sitter? Does the medium's mind extract the information, or does the sitter's mind offer it? How are relevant facts extracted from the mass of information available? Most importantly of all, if the mind really does possess these astonishing facilities, why do they not manifest themselves more widely and more often? Is it reasonable to postulate that an entranced medium is capable of extracting specific facts from a sitter, an unknown living person, or from a universal data-bank, when he has no conscious knowledge of doing so?

The answer that springs immediately to mind in response to all of these questions is, of course, 'No, it is not reasonable,' but in this particular instance such an answer can only lead to deeper and yet muddier mental waters for, if the medium is *not* utilizing extraordinary and unsuspected powers that are available to him, apparently, due to his disassociated mental state, then he is certainly engaging in telepathic communication with persons known to be deceased, because that option is, in the light of all the evidence, the only one remaining. As options go, it is not particularly reasonable either!

Of all the theories, and on the evidence, the occult theory fares best, because it seems to cover all the facts. This is not particularly surprising, because occultism by its nature has had to develop ideas as to the etheric and astral underpinnings of material existence, and has consequently managed to cover all eventualities fairly reasonably when it comes to apparitions. This, however, does not mean that occultists are cleverer than other people, or even that the occult theory is right. We have seen that what is required is a hypothesis regarding a subtle environment that underlies the physical. Occultism has certainly developed such a hypothesis, but so have other people — and it must be said that those hypotheses, unlike that favoured by occultists, are not based on mystical systems that cannot be orally transmitted, but only personally realized.

From this evaluation of current theories, it could easily

appear that our chances of understanding the cause and nature of apparitions — or of really proving survival of death — in the near future are poor, because, effectively, we are back where we started. All the theories are imperfect — either they do not fit every fact, or they do not cover every eventuality, or they stretch credulity to the limit, or they are not susceptible of proof — and yet none can be altogether discarded because we do not know the parameters of extra-sensory perception, the capabilities of the human mind, or the constitution of the human spirit. Also, and very importantly, portions of theory sometimes do fit portions of fact, or whole theories whole cases. One vital point, therefore, has been established, and that is that it is most unwise to attempt to make any one theory fit every event. A flexible mental attitude, it seems, is essential until further evidence and new facts are to hand. Until then all theories must remain speculative, and all things possible.

— *Part 3* —

PRACTICALITIES

— *11* —

Investigation

So many cases, so many people, so many experiences. So many different reactions, so many conflicting opinions. And yet so many likenesses so far as type of experience and type of reaction is concerned, and so easily may even conflicting opinions be reconciled. 'Ghosts' are proven to exist, people see and experience them, not always completely subjectively. Such things really are. But we do not understand what or why they are, and unfortunately unless the facts about these things are more widely accepted; unless the things themselves continue to be investigated, as thoroughly and scientifically as possible, attitudes toward them will remain as primitive as they are today and the 'why' and 'what' will remain shrouded in mystery. Sadly, public opinion is not changed overnight — and the investigator's task is not a simple one.

Assume, for a moment, as every investigator must, that a report of a paranormal experience is not what it seems; that the experience it relates to is, in fact, not paranormal at all, but on the contrary quite ordinary. How then might that experience be explained away? Might it perhaps be illusory? Might it have some perfectly mundane cause? Might the percipient have misinterpreted what he has seen or heard? Could an apparent apparition be the result of mistaken identity on the part of the percipient? Has the percipient exaggerated what he has seen or in any way distorted the evidence given to the investigator? Has the percipient deliberately hoaxed the investigator, or been himself the victim of a hoax? And if any of these things are applicable, how and why are they so?

The purpose of every investigator is to arrive at the truth, whatever the truth may be, and the first axiom of psychical research is that a very large percentage of all reported, researched and recorded cases of allegedly paranormal phenomena turn out to be due either to natural causes or to human intervention — which means, to put it crudely (and rather simplistically), that much of it can be put down to things like plumbing, climatic conditions, small boys, and out and out fraud, and that the investigator will spend quite a lot of time examining and thinking about things far removed from the paranormal: the vagaries of someone else's plumbing, or the possible motives of his witness, for example.

The small percentage of cases that remain, albeit genuine enough, are some of them wholly subjective, and all affected by a multiplicity of factors so complex in their causes and effects that the investigator frequently experiences great difficulty in extracting even the most basic facts of the experience.

'Evidence' of any kind is liable to distortion, even when it does not relate to so emotive a subject as psychical phenomena, (a) because few people are as observant as they might be, and (b) because every individual perceives events in relation to his own life, beliefs and knowledge, and in accordance with his mental abilities. Thus 'reality' — that exceedingly complex structure — is inevitably strained through the muslin of personal bias when it comes to providing 'evidence' of anything seen or experienced, and all evidential statements, of whatever nature, contain distortions of reality.

A witness to an allegedly paranormal event will make a statement as to what G.W. Lambert in his lecture 'The Use of the Evidence in Psychical Research' calls the *primary effects* (by which he means the apparition or other sensory phenomena), but that statement will also contain *secondary effects* which will consist of what the witness has made of what he saw, or heard, or felt. Those secondary effects will include exaggerations, distortions, errors in memory, and not least the witness's attempts to rationalize what he has experienced. They will, in other words, be an *interpretation* of the truth, rather than the truth itself.

Take, for example, the case of a taxi-driver who has been asked to give a formal report of an accident he has witnessed. The accident is a serious one, and the report is to be used in evidence by the insurance company acting on behalf of the victim. That person, a woman, has been badly injured, and might as a consequence be crippled for the rest of her life. The taxi-driver has been driving professionally in one or another capacity for some 33 years. He drives well and carefully, and has long experience behind him. This is not the first accident he has seen, and only one of many that he has managed to avoid being directly involved in. But what is this experience worth to the insurance company, which is looking for as

realistic an assessment of events as it can come by? Certainly
the taxi-driver was present at the site of the accident at the
time it took place. Certainly he saw the victim lying in the
road. But he was also driving a vehicle in the dark on a narrow,
unlit, country lane when he came upon the accident; he met
with it suddenly and simultaneously as he drove over the brow
of a hill; and he had to think quickly in order to avoid being
involved in the accident himself together with his passenger
— to think about the position of his own vehicle and of the
other vehicles in front and behind him, about the width of the
verges, the position of oncoming traffic, the distance away and
depth of the ditches at either side of the road, and his chances
of getting his vehicle over such a ditch rather than into it were
such a course to prove necessary. He did not see how the
victim came to be lying in the road. He did not see how the
other cars involved in the accident came to be arranged in
the pattern they had assumed on the road. And so, effectively,
he saw and experienced nothing of the accident, save those
aspects of it that related directly to himself, because he was
not expecting it and did not have time to observe it objectively
when it happened. He saw and spoke to many people at the
site of the accident. Would he know them if he saw them
now? Could he recall with any accuracy what they said to
him, and he to them? Could he describe the colours of the
scene, the paintwork of the cars, the subtle hues of hair and
complexion? Or could he relate only what he *felt*, what he
thought, what he *personally experienced*?

The percipient of a spontaneous hallucination of any kind is
in much the same position. He comes upon what appears to
be an apparition, say, suddenly and without warning; he does
not expect to see it, and his mind is fully occupied with other
things. Once he has perceived it, his body may freeze, but his
mind will race. Automatically he will commence speculating,
questioning, intellectualizing — absolutely subjectively —
about his experience, what it means for him, and what he is
going to do about it. The result is that he in fact notices very
little — consciously at least — that does not relate directly to
himself. He will, for example, be able to describe his own
sensations minutely, but he may not be able to recall in any
detail either the appearance or actions of the other protagonist
in the drama. While he is thinking about his experience
afterwards he may, to be sure, 'remember' factors that he had
forgotten or did not realize that he had seen, but what is the
inherent value of these 'memories'? How accurate are they?
How dependent upon what he has thought about since, or the
remarks and questions and attitudes of other people? If, for

example, he states that he saw an apparition open a door and walk through it, did he in fact see just that — the apparition pulling open the door and going through it — or did his mind, perplexed perhaps by the sudden presence and subsequent disappearance of his uninvited guest, supply logical factors in reality missing from the experience, in order to normalize and so legitimize it to some extent?

Simple errors of observation are common, as are misinterpretations of what is actually seen or heard. Misinterpretation in particular is a simple matter. Let us go back to our taxi-driver. When he first left his car at the site of the accident, he observed that the victim was lying in the middle of the road. He also observed a car, damaged at the front on the driver's side, slewed across the road, with the door on the driver's side open, and another car, at right angles to the first, also damaged on the driver's side. Both cars were empty. By the side of the road, a small group of people stood huddled together. Two other people crouched over the victim. From these facts, the taxi-driver assumed that the victim had been run over whilst crossing the road, and that the driver of the car who had collided with her, had also collided with another vehicle as he swerved in an attempt to avoid her. These assumptions were logical in the light of what he saw, but were not correct. In fact the woman had been the driver of the first car, had lost control of it, and had attempted to leap to safety when she saw that an accident was inevitable. Neither had she been run over by the second car, with which her vehicle had collided. Instead, she was hit by a third car, a vehicle that had been behind hers when she lost control of it, and which was now drawn to the side of the road. Despite his experience then, the taxi-driver found it easy to misinterpret what he saw, and because he did so, all his assumptions about the event proved wrong. Had he not spoken to other drivers at the scene of the accident, and discovered the relative truth of the matter, what use then would his version of events have been? What use, indeed, are they now, modified as they are by the thoughts, experiences and beliefs of other people?

So it is with the percipients of paranormal phenomena, whether genuine or not. If the witness is alone when he experiences the phenomena, then he will make assumptions that might be as wildly incorrect as those of the taxi-driver. If the experience is collective, the percipients will turn to each other to discuss it, and so their own experience, their own assumptions, will be immediately modified, just as the experience of the taxi-driver was modified by that of the other people present at the site of the accident.

Most people tend to make assumptions from facts as they see them, and events as they experience them, in precisely this way, and most, too, tend to mentally correlate the unknown and unidentified with the known and recognized, particularly when it comes to 'noises off', as it were. Thus at night any bush becomes a bogle, and if any noise remotely resembling footsteps is heard at any time, then footsteps that noise will become. Whole trains of inference might arise from a single such mistaken premise, and they prove very difficult to unravel. Let it not be forgotten either, that it is not unknown for an individual to spontaneously construct a phantom to go with those inexplicable 'footsteps', or that subjective apparitional phenomena seem to be highly contagious. (Anyone who has difficulty in believing that it is possible to construct a phantom should refer to the case of 'Philip, the Phantom Phantom', a being invented and constructed in 1972 by members of the Toronto Society for Psychical Research, which became a very interesting and very physical presence indeed.)

In some cases, too, an individual reporting allegedly paranormal phenomena might desire or actually *need* to hoax an investigator, and in others a person or persons unknown might have reason to hoax the percipient. Sometimes, also, the odd percipient might mistake the identity of the person he saw, and go on thereafter to misinterpret what occurred. Taken in the round, the available evidence does not support the premise that very many cases result of deliberate hoaxing or mistaken identity, but misinterpretation, lack of observation, and exaggeration of the evidence are usually present in every case.

So the percipient is prone to error, accidental or deliberate: his version of events must be approached with care, and the investigator must first extract the wheat from the chaff and then examine what remains with great care, taking nothing for granted, accepting no statement at face value. What does this mean in practice?

Effectively, it means that the primary effects of the witness's story must be first extricated from the rest of his statement and then deliberately stripped of all the most obvious inferences that he might have drawn from them. It also means that those primary effects must be carefully evaluated, because some primary effects are more likely to mean that the phenomenon is *not* paranormal than others.

For example, a witness states that he heard footsteps, followed directly afterwards by the sound of a woman's dress sweeping the floor. He saw nothing, and on examination found that he was alone in the house. From these factors he assumes that his experience was paranormal, and that his house is haunted. The investigator, however, can assume nothing of the kind. He knows only that the witness heard a sound like footsteps, and that this sound was followed by another that resembled the sound of a woman's dress. All the rest is inference, and must be recognized as such. The witness may add that he experienced the same effects on a subsequent occasion, but that these were then accompanied by fear, horror, or a feeling of cold on his part. The fresh effects that form part of the second experience would seem to cast a new light on the whole matter, to make it more 'real' as it were, but in fact they do not, because where the primary effect is an unaccountable noise, the phenomena are more likely than not to be based in a mundane cause. The witness has heard a noise resembling footsteps, followed by further sounds resembling the sweep of a woman's dress on the ground. From this his mind has made a series of assumptions: for him, footsteps equals person, dress equals female person. However, he has seen nothing, has searched the house, has found no one. Hence his mind has presented him with a new equation: footsteps plus dress equals woman, woman minus physical presence equals 'ghost' — and this is more likely to have caused the feeling of cold and fear than anything else. Unfortunately, once having reached that point, anything might happen, including the appearance of an apparition to go with the footsteps. This would be a purely subjective construct, but it would still be there, and part of the investigator's problem — a problem that would probably be compounded by the very human tendency to begin a story at its most interesting and impressive point. Our imaginary witness would be unlikely to tell his story in chronological order as we have examined it here: he would begin with the 'ghost' — for him the most important and evidential part of his experience — and only much patience and many questions would have allowed the investigator to discover that this phantom was a *secondary* rather than a *primary* effect. Of course, until the investigator has extracted the primary effect of any experience, he is in a poor position to look for causes.

Causes fall into two main categories: *mechanical* and *personal*. Mechanical causes are impersonal and unintentional: creaking woodwork, faulty plumbing, car headlights, small birds and animals. Personal causes are those which originate with living people or with apparitions and other sensory hallucinations. The difficulty is to assign effect to cause. In the case of our imaginary witness, the investigator, concentrating on the primary effect — 'unaccountable noise' — would seek mechanical causes for that noise in the first instance, because if he could account for the noise (and reproduce it to order) he could account for all the other effects too.

Had the primary effect in our example been an apparition, unaccompanied by any other effects, then the case would have been very different, but still much would have rested on the witness's description of the apparition. As stated in Chapter Four, all paranormal experiences are particularly vivid and memorable, leaving the witness with lasting images and impressions. These suffer distortion in the course of time, but they do not fade, and the witness's description of them will retain the impact of his first impression. Where the impression is lifelike and detailed, however incomplete (as Louisa Scott's impression of the clergyman on the haunted road was incomplete), then the experience is likely to have been a telepathic one. Where it is vague and ill-defined, or suggests some archetypal image, then it is probably subjective. Had our imaginary witness really come up with a phantom to accompany his footsteps, then this would have been a vague image, constructed from the 'information' he had to hand. His phantom would have been a woman dressed in a long gown, because that is the image directly suggested by the noises he heard, and because of the tendency to produce archetypal figures under such circumstances, it would probably also have been gowned in black, and heavily veiled to boot.

What of the investigator in all of this? As part of every investigation, he must attempt to either reproduce the phenomena or experience them for himself, but the investigator is a human being too, and what applies to the percipient, applies equally to him. If the phenomena turn out to be really paranormal, what then? How good is the investigator's evidence likely to be in the event that he is lucky enough to experience it for himself? Happily, and because forewarned is forearmed, rather better than that of the original percipient, but still, of course, imperfect. In real-life situations, knowledge of human nature and how various kinds of phenomena are likely to behave is not enough to eliminate error. Thus it is always best if a case is investigated by more than one person. Indeed, a party of four or five people working together is the most desirable way. Firstly, of course, a single person working alone cannot be everywhere at once, and cannot keep his eye on everything. Secondly, the more witnesses there are to anything that might occur the better — always, assuming, of course, that the investigator applies his controls as stringently to himself and the rest of his party as he should to his witness.

Every investigation should follow the same well-defined and orderly course. Certain procedures must be followed, and they should be carried out properly, conscientiously, in a specific order and — if the results are to be of any value at all — very, very carefully. Thus the investigator must:

1. Interview the witness(es).
2. Visit the site and examine, photograph, and sketch it.
3. Obtain signed statements from the witness(es).
4. Make a thorough investigation of the site.
5. Question the witness(es).
6. If the phenomena are alleged to occur frequently, attempt to witness them himself.
7. Make a formal statement and append it to the witness's own statement.

In addition, if he is one of a party of people who are working an investigation together, he must help to draw up a plan of campaign which must be strictly adhered to. One of the investigators should agree to be in charge, for a situation where there are too many chiefs and no indians will result in chaos and achieve nothing.

Over the next chapters we will be looking in detail as to how all these matters may best be handled, but before we go on to do that it is necessary to make one or two very important points about investigation in general and witnesses in particular.

For the investigator, the investigation is likely to be interesting and fun — and that holds true even where the phenomena turn out to be rooted in very mundane causes. For the witness, however, the phenomena are not fun, and probably not particularly interesting either. For him it is at very least a pain in the neck and is more likely to be an irritating, worrying and frightening intrusion into his life. The investigator is going to have to ask him some very awkward questions and, if the phenomena happen to centre around him or his house, then he is going to have to invade his premises, his home. It is therefore important that the investigator should try not to behave like an insensitive ass! He should be friendly and relaxed, and try to include the witness (wherever possible) in his plans. Obviously, if he thinks a fraud is being perpetrated for whatever reason, this can be a little difficult, but he should at least still try. As you will see, there can be a good many reasons for people attempting to perpetrate a fraud of this kind, and any investigator should try to get under the witness's skin to see his point of view before making value judgements about him in his own mind and reflecting them through his behaviour.

Remember, too, that however interesting real phenomena are to outsiders, the victims are only really interested in getting rid of them. If that is the case, and the witnesses are living in a state of morbid terror, no one should prolong their agony. Further, no one should try to help them out by becoming involved in do-it-yourself exorcism. The investigator might call in a clergyman or he might call in a medium (depending, of course, on the witness's beliefs and preferences), but unless he is in either of those lines of work himself, he should not simply take it upon himself to buy a book and get on with it, because this may (in fact it almost certainly will!) make matters much, much worse.

— *12* —

Interviewing Witnesses

The first, and most important, part of any investigation is the preliminary interview of the witness or witnesses, and this should, if possible, take place where the alleged phenomena took place, so as to enable the investigator to have a look round the site and complete his preliminary investigation of that, too.

So far as the investigator is concerned, the interview has a dual purpose: it must reveal (a) what the witness has experienced, and (b) what the witness is like — what he thinks, what his circumstances are, what the state of his mental and physical health might be, what his motive is in approaching the investigator. This is a tall order, and every effort should therefore be made to ensure that the occasion runs as smoothly and efficiently as possible.

To complete a preliminary interview and site examination the investigator will need: a pen, notebook, tape recorder, graph-lined notebook, measuring tape and camera. (A simple and inexpensive camera equipped with a flash is all that is really necessary, although obviously sophisticated equipment is likely to produce better results. Advice on the film, shutter speeds, and techniques applicable to specific problems can usually be obtained from your photographic supplier. Most such stores are either owned by, or employ, a 'camera buff' who will be interested in the technical difficulties presented by psychical research, and may in some cases be willing to lend equipment or services.)

Because the witness should not be interrupted *at all* once he has commenced describing his experience, the investigator should check that his tape recorder is working before he leaves home, and again before the witness begins his story. He should make such notes as occur to him during the course of the narrative as inconspicuously as possible, and preferably out of the witness's direct line of sight. It is very important that the investigator ask no questions of the witness at this stage, and that he make every effort to ensure that he does not lead the witness at all. This is because questions asked at this juncture, whilst almost certainly clarifying matters for the investigator, often lead the witness to embroider his experience both by reference to the questions asked and by the investigator's reactions to his answers. As already pointed out, the witness will have already (unavoidably) embroidered his account more than one would wish. As the investigation progresses, further embellishment will occur in any event, but if the investigator restrains himself from asking questions or breaking into the witness's narrative in any way at this early stage, he will at least have the benefit of a record of the experience as the witness originally interpreted it to which he can afterwards refer.

When the witness's narrative draws to a natural conclusion, he should be asked to write out his account, and date and sign it. The investigator ought, of course, to have a good narrative record on tape, but in case of mechanical failure the written record will serve as evidence of the preliminary interview. The witness *need* not write out his account on the spot whilst the investigator is waiting, but it is in many ways better that he *should* do so, for obvious reasons.

At this juncture, the investigator can go on to ask questions of his own. Some of those questions will relate directly to the narrative he has just heard, and will be prompted by it. Others, however, are standard questions that will be germane in every case. Here is a representative list of such questions:

1. When did you first see/hear/feel the 'ghost'/have this experience? (Obtain the date and the time as nearly as can be estimated.)
2. Were you alone at the time? If you were not, who was with you? (Obtain names and addresses.)
3. Did your companion(s), if any, also experience the phenomena in any way?
4. Would he/she/they be willing to make a statement?
5. How many times have you experienced the phenomena since? (Obtain dates and times.)
6. Did it/they behave in the same way on every occasion?
7. Where exactly did you experience the phenomena? (Obtain as exact a description as possible.)
8. How far away from you was the figure?/How far were you from the source of the sound?

9. If you have experienced this phenomenon more than once, did you always experience it in the same place?
10. Did the figure appear gradually or suddenly?
11. How long did the phenomena endure?
12. What was the lighting at the time?
13. Was there a mirror anywhere near, or a window, or any other reflective surface?
14. Please describe the figure/noise/sensation.
15. Did the figure appear to be solid or transparent?
16. Was the appearance coloured, or black and white?
17. What was the figure wearing?
18. Did you recognize the figure/voice as being that of someone you know or have known, or have you been able to identify the figure from a photograph or some other source since your experience?
19. If you recognized the person as being someone you know or have known, had that person been much in your thoughts of late?
20. Did the figure/presence speak to you, or make any attempt to speak to you, or make any gesture of any kind?
21. If it did speak, what did it say?
22. Did you speak to the figure/answer the voice?
23. If so, what was its reaction, if any?
24. What was your immediate reaction to the phenomenon?
25. How did you feel when you experienced it? Frightened? Sad? Surprised? Glad?
26. Did the figure act naturally?
27. How did the figure disappear? Suddenly? Or did it just fade slowly away?
28. Did you feel any variation in temperature before or after you saw the figure, or while it was present?
29. Did you notice anything else unusual at the time? Sudden intense quiet? Unusual sounds?
30. Were you asleep or nearly so at the commencement of the experience?
31. If you were asleep, what woke you up?
32. If you were awake when the experience commenced, what was your state of mind? Relaxed? Tense? Apprehensive?
33. What were you doing at the time? If you were reading/thinking, what were you reading/thinking about?
34. How did you feel directly after the experience?
35. Did you feel any change in the atmosphere of the place afterwards? Was it lighter, darker, warmer, colder?

36. Did you have an animal with you when you had the experience? If so, how did it react?
37. Does the building or place have the reputation of being haunted? If it does, when did you discover this? (Obtain dates if possible.) Was it before or after the experience? How long before/after?
38. Have you had previous experiences of this kind? (Obtain complete details, with dates.)
39. Do you know anyone else who has had similar experiences? If so, are you related to that person? (Obtain degree of relationship.)

Once the investigator has obtained the answers to these questions and any others which might have reference to the witness's narrative — all these should, obviously, be taped or otherwise recorded — he will have completed the first part of his interview with the witness and (hopefully) obtained a good, clear, evidential account of what the witness experienced. He will not, however, be able to draw any conclusions from what he has heard, and ought in fact to restrain himself from forming even the most tentative opinion, because his record is far from complete. Later, he will be able to unite the information gained from this part of the interview with other facts about the witness and the site. For the time being, however, he must proceed to fulfil the second purpose of the interview, and try to find out more about the witness as a person.

This is not a simple matter, because it is no longer possible for the investigator to simply ask a series of straightforward questions of his witness. Certain facts must certainly be laid bare, but these are facts about the witness's private life, and he will probably not feel them to be germane to his experience. It is therefore up to the investigator to lead the conversation as tactfully as possible, and encourage the witness to talk about himself and his circumstances, and so tell or show him what he wants to know. Here is a representative list of 'unaskable' questions, together with the reasons why the investigator must, somehow, discover the answers to them:

1. Were you feeling well at the time of the experience?
2. Do you suffer from any chronic illness? Diabetes? Bronchitis? Any intestinal ailment?
3. Are you taking any medication at all? If so, what is it?
4. Is there any history of epilepsy in your family?

Epilepsy and the experience of paranormal phenomena appear to be linked. Such experiences are not necessarily a result of the disease, but the disease may in some way be a predisposing factor. Serious diseases of the lungs (particularly tuberculosis) have been linked to auditory and other hallucinations, and in such cases 'paranormal' experiences are frequently a result of the disease. The fever associated with some illnesses, even commonplace ones like influenza, can actually cause hallucinations; but fever can produce an altered state of consciousness that is a predisposing factor to the experience of them, too. Some intestinal ailments have been linked with telekinesis, but where the disease is the cause of this effect, the effect is likely to lessen and finally disappear as the patient recovers.

Some types of medication (particularly antihistamines and tranquillizers) have side-effects which may cause some patients to suffer hallucinations. Remember that such medication may be a predisposing factor.

5. Did you have a headache at the time of the experience or develop a headache directly after the experience?

Constant headaches are sometimes symptomatic of serious diseases, which may cause hallucinations. Migraine headaches are a genetic associate of epilepsy and sometimes involve auditory and other hallucinations. Where undeveloped or 'natural' mediumship is assisting the production of the phenomena, the medium frequently suffers a severe headache coupled with a feeling of debility when the experience is over.

6. Do you have good eyesight? Do you wear glasses or contact lenses? Are you long or short-sighted? Are you colour blind?
7. If you normally wear glasses or other aids to vision, were you wearing them at the time of the experience?
8. If you normally wear glasses or other aids to vision and were not wearing them at the time you saw the figure, does it occur to you in retrospect that your eyesight seemed to be better on that occasion than it normally is or should have been?

It is important to work out how good the witness's vision really is. If, for example, he has recently obtained a new prescription, or is wearing unfamiliar aids to vision (bi-focals, for example), or has just commenced wearing contact lenses, this may be the direct and simple cause of the hallucination. If, on the other hand, he has seen a well-defined figure clearly that would under normal circumstances have been difficult for him to see, either because it was too close, or too far away, or because he was not wearing his glasses, then the hallucination might have been the externalized result of a telepathic 'prompt', and is likely in any event to be objective, rather than subjective, in nature. A person with poor eyesight who is not wearing any aid to vision at the time of his experience is more likely to misinterpret what he sees than a normally sighted person.

9. Do you drink/take drugs at all? Infrequently? Fairly frequently? Regularly?
10. Had you been drinking/taking drugs at all on the day you experienced the phenomena? Had you drunk excessively the day before?
11. Have you ever taken hallucinogenic drugs for any reason?

Some of the reasons for these questions are obvious. If your witness is a dipsomaniac then hallucinations are his everyday fare, but even quite moderate drinking can cause such effects in some people. Alcohol remains in the bloodstream for some considerable time after its consumption. The greater the consumption the greater the length of time required for the body to dispose of the alcohol — and the greater the chance of its reacting with some other, perhaps otherwise harmless, ingested substance to produce those physical effects which cause hallucinations. Most proscribed substances can cause hallucinations, although not all are termed 'hallucinogenic'. True hallucinogens (LSD, for example) can remain in the system for many months, causing hallucinations that occur without warning long after the drug was taken.

12. Are you currently employed? If not, how long have you been out of work?
13. Do you enjoy your work?
14. Must you travel far to work?
15. Do you like your workmates?

Details of the witness's employment can prove to be a very useful source of information. The average fully-employed person spends seven or more hours of his day actually working, and up to three hours travelling to and from work, and it is a singularly fortunate person who wholeheartedly enjoys his work, feels himself to be adequately paid for it, and is never bored or troubled by his job, his workmates, or his work environment.

How bored, how dissatisfied, how troubled, is the witness by his employment — or, of course, his lack of it? How might these emotions manifest themselves? A busy, involved, happy person has a very different outlook to one who is genuinely and deeply dissatisfied with his working life, and whose mind may consequently be either occupied with perpetual worry or more or less at a permanent loose end. Every human being needs to feel needed, to know that he is performing some function that is more or less essential in the larger scheme of things. The feeling of being simply a number, unimportant, overlooked and absolutely replaceable can create a very real need to be interesting, to be the centre of attention, to attract notice in some way, to be different and somehow meaningful.

16. Are you happy in your home life?
17. Have you a good social life?
18. Have you any hobbies? If so, what are they?

Most people find their *raison d'être* at home or, if they live alone, in their friends, hobbies, and social life, and are important, meaningful, and well thought of in those areas, whatever their working environment has to offer. But this happy state of affairs does not apply to everyone, and therefore every effort must be made to arrive at some concrete and well-supported conclusion about the quality of the witness's home and/or social life. The investigator should observe the attitude of the family members (if any) towards the witness, and his toward them, and listen to what he has to say about his friends and the ways in which he spends his spare time. Does the family seem to be a close-knit unit or does there seem to be any discord between family members? Is there any obvious animosity or other negative emotion directed toward any one individual, and if there is, is that individual the witness? Does the witness seem to have few, or no, friends? Is the witness's hobby one which can or must be pursued alone?

It is not at all unusual for an individual seeking to inject meaning into his life and inspire interest in others to seek these things — often unconsciously — through occultism; and it is not unusual either for such desires to manifest themselves in apparently inexplicable psychic phenomena that are just as likely to be genuine as fraudulent. The conditions that surround the witness at home and at work might therefore constitute important evidential clues in some instances.

Another point to consider:

19. Has the family endured any unusually stressful events in the last six months?

If the family as a unit has been subjected to any out of the way or stressful events of recent date, for example, a death in the family, or a divorce, this could seriously affect the state of mind of all its members, albeit in very different ways. Such events can, for instance, create feelings of guilt which, although baseless, are nonetheless very real, and such feelings can result in the appearance of phenomena which are temporary, but nevertheless disturbing.

20. What are your assets and financial status?
21. How do you feel about publicity?

If the phenomena centre about the witness or the witness's home, some effort must be made to find out what the witness's interest is in the house he lives in, as well as his feelings about it. Is he an owner-occupier? A private sector tenant? A council tenant? Is he living with his parents or other relatives, and if so, why? Is he a minor? Has he perhaps found it difficult to find accommodation of his own for himself and his family?

If the witness is an owner-occupier, then he is extremely unlikely to be seeking publicity of any kind, if only because the only thing more difficult to sell than a haunted house is second-hand underwear. If, on the other hand, he is a private sector tenant, then he might well have all kinds of reasons for seeking publicity in this particular way. Revenge on the landlord, for instance, for what is hard to sell is equally difficult to let, or perhaps a place on the council housing list. Councils will house individuals who are 'homeless' for whatever reason — and well-publicized 'ghosts' have frequently provided quite an acceptable reason for homelessness, or proved to be a quick way out of property that is too small, badly maintained, or in some other way inconvenient. The investigator should therefore be aware this his testimony may be the necessary prerequisite to the witness obtaining housing more to his taste, even where the phenomena themselves are quite genuine.

There is no better key to the motives of a witness than a simple question as to his attitude toward publicity. What does he feel about newspaper or television coverage of his experiences? Is he horrified? Or is he perhaps quite pleased? Has he already approached a newspaper or any other media vehicle? Why has he approached the investigator? Is he expecting him to publicize his experiences? Does he need money, and is he expecting payment from the investigator or from any other source? Is he a publican, restaurateur, or the owner or proprietor of any other business which might benefit from rumour of a 'ghost' on the premises?

The witness's answers to these questions will certainly provide very strong pointers to his attitude and motives. Not very many people in a situation involving real phenomena actually enjoy publicity. The whole affair is too painful, too frightening, too inconvenient and too likely to make fools of them. Really they would just like it to go away. Witnesses who appear to be looking forward to the publication of their woes usually have an axe to grind somewhere — and it is, of course, up to the investigator to find out what that axe might be. Possible property 'wangles', the existence of private feuds, and any business need for publicity of any kind are good reasons for the investigator to be wary of getting involved in any overt desire for publicity on the part of the witness (although if the Press are already involved it is best to actively seek their assistance and co-operation than otherwise, despite the fact that the presence of media personnel in and around the focus of the phenomena can so alter conditions as to have an adverse effect on the collection of evidence).

It is worth remembering, too, that any landlord is well within his rights to sue an individual whose behaviour is calculated to lower or destroy the value of his or her property. The law in England is property-oriented, and damages could be substantial, whether an investigator is able to produce reasonable evidence to support his allegations or not.

To sum up: the investigator must acquire knowledge as to the witness's experience(s) and as to the witness himself during the course of this preliminary interview. He needs, in other words, to be able to construct a psychological profile as well as a factual account. Because the investigator must also do some preliminary work on the site during the course of the initial interview, a great many of the questions relating to the witness's personal life can be worked into general conversation while he gets on with that work. Some questions, however, cannot — and yet they must be asked. The most difficult is here left until the last:

22. Are you now receiving, or have you ever received, psychiatric care? If so, when, and why?

This is a very difficult question to ask of anyone, but it is a very important one, simply because the investigator must know whether or not his witness is in any way mentally disturbed. The answer will obviously colour the results of the entire investigation, but the investigator must just as obviously use his common sense. The witness might have received psychiatric care for simple common ailments like depression, anxiety attacks or asthma, none of which are known to actually cause hallucinations, and which might well have no bearing on the matter at hand. It is as well to keep this in mind.

— *13* —

Sites

Once the first part of the preliminary interview with the witness is complete, the investigator can go on to make a preliminary survey of the site. Site analysis is effectively the equivalent of the edging to the jigsaw puzzle of investigation — it is the parametrizing principle as well as the theatre of events. As you probably know, all jigsaw puzzles are best completed from the edge in, and so far as investigation is concerned, site examination is in many ways the place where the real work begins.

If the witness's experience took place out of doors, in a field or a wood perhaps, or whilst he was walking or driving home, then the investigator will obviously proceed rather differently than had the phenomena manifested inside a building. In either event, however, he should commence by making a scale plan of the site using a piece of graph paper, photographing the site extensively, and looking for prima-facie evidence that the phenomena might have been due to natural causes. Thus the witness should be asked to identify, if possible, his exact position within the landscape or building when the phenomena occurred. If he saw an apparition, he should identify as nearly as possible its exact position too. If the experience was auditory, then he should identify the direction from which the sound came. If an apparition moved through the landscape or building, its route should be established. Once these details have been dealt with, the investigator needs to measure and photograph the site from every angle, so as to produce a scale plan of the relative positions of witness and apparition and every other object of note within the immediate area, together with a set of corresponding photographs, so that this information may be examined in the light of the witness's statement. The map in Chapter Seven, page 58, is an example of such plans.

1. Working Out of Doors.

When psychical phenomena have been experienced out of doors, the first step is to look for natural features in the landscape which might have a bearing on the witness's statement. Trees, telegraph poles, rocks, stones, washing lines, road signs — all these can, in certain circumstances, be misinterpreted, and therefore cannot be ignored.

For example, washing flapping about on somebody's clothes line can, on a dark or misty evening, look sufficiently otherworldly to give someone a nasty start — particularly if the washing in question happens to be attached to a solitary house on a lonely and unlit country road. Most householders do their weekly wash on the same day every week, which gives the phenomena the repetitive flavour of a genuine haunting, and it wouldn't be the first time that a few sheets had formed the basis of a modern legend.

Another example: a road sign near my home is sited in a slight dip in the road at a spot where Savernake Forest drops away into farmland. I know that the road sign is there. I have seen it in daylight and in darkness and in all weather conditions over a period of more than three years. It is a triangular sign that stands on a round pole of sufficient length to make it much taller than a man, and indeed it looks nothing at all like a man. Nevertheless, once in a while, and in the right conditions, it continues to fool me into thinking that it is a man, and a very large man at that, and on those occasions it never fails to bring my heart into my mouth. The colours of twilight, the rising mist, the atmosphere and reputation of the forest, and possibly the very contours of the road, all contrive to lend a depth and dimension to that simple sign that do not in reality exist. Even the most normal and everyday objects should not therefore be ignored or discounted.

2. Working Indoors.

Working inside buildings is more complicated than working out of doors, simply because there are so many ways in which the building itself might have caused apparently paranormal phenomena. This applies to new as well as old premises. Because buildings are sometimes at the root of the witness's problem, once the investigator has completed his interview, established the exact positions of all the protagonists in the drama, taken his photographs and carefully completed his scale plan, he must ask a further series of questions, and use his eyes and his common sense to check as best he can the structure of the building he is working in and the environment in which it stands. Here is a representative list of the sort of questions that might prove useful, together with some of the reasons why they need to be asked:

1. Is the building detached? If it is not, what does the witness know about the surrounding houses?
2. Are the premises close to a road? If they are, what kind of traffic travels along the road, and is the road, in the witness's opinion, sufficiently good to bear the weight of traffic?
3. Is the house situated on or near a railway line?
4. If the house is isolated, does it have mains drainage?
5. How old is the building?
6. What is it constructed of?
7. Has central heating recently been installed? Does the witness know if it has recently been installed in neighbouring premises? If any heating has been freshly installed, was this a professional job?
8. Has fresh insulation recently been installed? Or a damp course? Has any such been installed in the neighbouring premises? If so, when?
9. If no damp course has been installed of late, does one exist at all?
10. Have any repairs been done on the house? If so, what were they and when were they completed?
11. Has any furniture been imported into the premises? If so, which pieces and where are they?
12. How old is the plumbing? When was it installed? Has it been repaired or otherwise tampered with of late?
13. Most importantly, did the phenomena experienced precede the introduction of any of these possible changes in the interior environment of the house?
14. If the property is surrounded by trees or has roses or other flora growing up or over it, could this be the source of any tapping? Or might birds be the cause?
15. Is the cistern or any of the taps in the house leaking?
16. Where do the water pipes run in the house, and how old are they?
17. How is the water heated, and how old is that system?
18. Has double glazing been installed in the premises recently? If it has, was this work completed by a professional glazier or builder?
19. Are there fruit trees or chestnut trees near the house or any of the outhouses? If there are, might any bumps

complained of be caused by apples, etc., falling onto a
roof?

20. Does the witness or any neighbour own any animal (i.e.
a cat) which might be the cause of any of the noises
complained of? Are there any feral animals, such as
squirrels, etc., in the neighbourhood which might be the
cause of the problem?

21. Are there any children in the neighbourhood? If there
are, is the witness on good terms with them? Could the
phenomena be the result of a hoax of any kind?

22. Has any neighbour complained of phenomena similar to
that which the witness has experienced? If so, which
neighbour and when, and would that person be prepared
to speak to the interviewer?

Old timber-framed houses are in many ways more stable than
houses of more modern design and construction, simply
because they move within their environment more easily and
are built to suit that environment and not the whim of man.
Unfortunately, this same ease of movement and fitness for the
site can also cause problems — which usually manifest in a
crop of cracks, raps, creaks, knocks, groans and crepitations
that can be very unnerving because they reproduce so perfectly
the sort of phenomena usually associated with 'ghosts'.

Timber will regularly give out cracks and groans if the
temperature rises or drops even marginally either inside or
outside the house, or if it suddenly begins to rain after a long
dry spell, or if even a moderately warm day follows a few days
of steady rain, simply because it is natural to wood to expand
and contract in this way. Where a great deal of timber exists
in a building, particularly if that building is old, these cracks
can occur all over the house whenever the temperature
changes for any reason, and may seem alarmingly rhythmic
and regular. In many climates the temperature outside can
change very quickly, also more and more people nowadays are
investing in central heating systems of one kind or another,
installing these as fast as they can in moated manors, baronial
halls, little thatched cottages, miniature maisonettes, and
Uncle Tom Cobley and all. The weather we can do little about,
and most people get used to its effects on the houses they live
in very quickly, but the effects of central heating are quite
another matter.

Central heating is undoubtedly a blessing, as anyone will
agree who remembers (as I do!) the burn at the front freeze
down the back and let's get to bed in one flying leap effect of
living with coal fires; but when central heating is installed in

old property, its effects are frequently more chilling than warming. Newly-installed central heating definitely reaches the parts other fires do not reach, warming and drying the fabric of an old house as it has never been warmed and dried before. If the house is well-insulated (thatched cottages, for example, are very well insulated indeed), this can cause timber floorboards, beams and stair-treads to crack, firstly nearest the radiators, and then at regular intervals across the rooms and on the stairs. The effect is startlingly like that of a person walking through the rooms of the house and up and down the staircase, and as radiators usually operate on timer-switches, so the 'footsteps' regularly appear at specific times of the day, mimicking a 'haunt' very well indeed. Central heating, too, can cause heavy condensation in old and new houses alike. This may precipitate in all sorts of unlikely places, including neat little round puddles in the middle of the floor. These consistently 'materialize' at the same spot for obvious reasons and, of course, at regular intervals.

As the house gradually warms up and dries out thoroughly, both of these effects will be less marked, but they will never disappear completely, and they will always be more noticeable for at least a short time at the beginning and end of every winter — a further example of 'periodicity' very convincing to the person well up on fictional 'ghost lore'. Thick carpets and underlay will, of course, mitigate at least the sound effects considerably, but they will not dispel them altogether — and anyway the first thing the new owner of an old house usually does these days is to restore it as nearly as possible to its 'original' condition. In many cases, 'original' condition means well-disguised heating systems which can cause considerable disturbance to the fabric of the building — and the fabric of very old buildings is often a 'fill' of stones, pebbles and medieval refuse that will rattle and rustle until it settles again — and nice polished floorboards, which have probably not seen daylight since more reasonable owners could afford even a sack to cover them. It also means exposed beams, unblocked fire-places, lots and lots of nice atmospheric old furniture — Welsh dressers, vast scrub-topped kitchen tables and the like — and Victorian copper plumbing lovingly renovated and polished at vast cost.

If a beam has ever been covered with a coat of plaster, removing the plaster and pitching it to 'restore' it will cause the condition of the timber to alter drastically and suddenly, and odd noises will result.

If a fireplace has once been bricked over, unblocking it and sweeping the chimney will allow a current of air to enter the building and seek out nooks and crannies forbidden it for many years — again, odd noises will result.

Old 'cottage' furniture is made of wood, much of it probably once varnished or painted a sensible colour by one or another of its previous owners, and removed by a chemical process in order to make it desirable and saleable. The furniture will then have been coated several times with a petroleum-based furniture polish, the effect of which is to produce a sheen on the wood which, albeit temporary, is very like that produced by 200 years of industrious labour. The chemical process is a drying one and the polishing process is an oily one, the result being that the furniture will be 'noisy' until the wood is thoroughly 'soaked' with polish. This will *take* approximately 200 years of industrious labour! Moreover, antique furniture which has been French polished, or simply polished to a high gloss by generations of owners, does not like central heating, which may cause the wood to warp and the varnish to crack. Both these latter processes are 'noisy'.

Even the most modern plumbing 'gurgles' on occasion, due to air-locks in the pipes and various sundry other causes. Victorian plumbing, however beautifully and efficiently renovated, 'gurgles' a lot. A full orchestra tuning-up *may* make more and odder noises than those which can be emitted by Victorian plumbing in full cry, but it is a close run thing!

An important point to remember is that any and all of these things need not necessarily be due to works carried out, or furniture imported into, the witness's house. Sound carries through party walls and ceilings, and is often the less identifiable for being to some extent 'baffled' by those barriers. The root of the witness's problem may well lie in the flat upstairs or the house next door.

So much for the effects of modern building works in old premises. But what about those features, no longer necessary, which have been forgotten? The walls of even a modest Elizabethan house can be four or more feet thick. It is quite possible — and was frequently convenient — to insert a room into the ample space between the inner and outer skin of the house, ventilated via the outward-facing brickwork, and accessed via panelling or a fireplace, or to construct a staircase in the wall that commenced in one room or passageway and terminated either outside or somewhere on the floor above or below. Sometimes, too, in terraced property — even property of more recent date — cellars and roof-spaces were allowed to run the length of the terrace with few or no walls to divide one house from another. Such features as these are easily 'lost' or forgotten. Once the necessity for a secret room is gone, for example, or access to the cellar of a particular house has been blocked inside the house itself, it might lie hidden for many years — particularly if the property is not registered land and original Deeds have been mislaid — and while such features are sometimes rediscovered in the course of renovation, this is not always the case.

All of these hidden places, however, can provide a home for small animals, or a playground for children, the latter being more likely than adults both to actively look for such things and to be in a position to discover them accidentally. If there are noises emanating from within the walls, under the floors, or above the ceilings of a house, children playing or animals living in forgotten spaces might well be the cause — and neither species can be relied upon to tell the owners of the property that such spaces are there.

It should not be forgotten in any event that old buildings, particularly if they are thatched and/or timber-framed, whether blessed with unsuspected rooms or not, are usually home to living beings other than those actually engaged in paying the mortgage on the property, nor that these uninvited guests are capable of causing problems and worries out of all proportion to their size.

Woodworm, for instance, are obviously very fond of wood, as are death-watch beetles, and both are naturally delighted to fall in with a nice beam or two. Although the secret munchings of these little creatures are soundless to our ears, the results of any extensive deprecations most definitely are not. Even the largest staircase, the thickest oak beam, has a limited lifespan in the face of determined and large-scale snacking, and the sounds of incipient and final demise can be loud and extremely peculiar.

Birds, meanwhile, like a nice thatched roof full of nooks, crannies, ready-made nesting material and fat, juicy insects. Thatch is dry, besides, and very warm. Much rustling and some sighing noises are usually the result.

Mice like thatch, too, as well as the spacious skirting boards and convenient underfloor and in-wall access common to such old houses, and because they will eat literally almost anything and are small enough to utilize very narrow runs, the noises they create are not confined to the vague scrabblings one would expect. Mice have been known to eat the felt pads on piano wires, thus producing 'ghostly' (albeit rather atonal) music, and to run along bell-wires, the result of which was mysterious ringings.

Rats adore the septic tanks that usually accompany remote

homes, and are often drawn by dustbins and the like to actually take up residence within the house, or else under or near it, where it is warm and dry, and where scraps can be picked up fairly effortlessly. Foxes and badgers love dustbins, hen runs and nice covered outhouses, and are besides arch nocturnal rummagers. All of these creatures, and many others not mentioned here, are capable of creating sounds in and around the house which are in turn capable of misinterpretation — and such sounds can be surprisingly noticeable where the premises are isolated and therefore relatively free of traffic and other 'human habitation' noises.

Of course, all houses, whether old or new, are subject to the stress and strain of time, circumstance, and poor workmanship. If the plaster in a new house is improperly applied, for instance, or inadequately dried, or if a damp course is installed in an old house causing water to rise through the walls, then efflorescence may well result. If this does happen, then the plaster will eventually crumble and disintegrate openly, but before things get to that stage it will first give off a curious glow, and then burst forth in the form of a fluffy fungal growth that resembles very fine textured cotton-wool. If the problem or part of the problem complained of is therefore stated to be pale lights playing over a particular wall or walls, or mist-figures inside the house, then it is worth checking for efflorescence and asking whether a damp course has been installed in the past six to nine months, either in the witness's premises or in the house next door.

If double glazing is improperly installed, or sub-standard materials are used in the insulation, then air can travel between the panes, giving odd groaning noises as the immediate result. The timbers of doors and windows in newly-built modern houses or those used to replace pre-existing woodwork in old houses have sometimes not been properly treated or conditioned before they are installed, either because the builders are economizing, or because the DIY owner of the house was unaware that the wood needed to be treated when he bought the goods and installed them in his home. Where this is the case, time and weather will cause the new wood either to shrink or swell, so that the doors and windows of the premises warp and fall out of true. When that happens they either open of themselves, or unaccountably jam all the time.

All window glass eventually succumbs to gravity and begins to flow imperceptibly downward, but this only becomes obvious when the glass is old. Wartime glass, frequently distorted to begin with, distorts yet further. This can give the effect of faces at the window when the house is inspected from the outside.

The list of things that can create odd and apparently paranormal effects within a building is endless, and only the most common of them have been included here. The investigator can therefore ill afford to overlook anything at all when he is working indoors. Footsteps? Faces at the window? Shrieks in the night? Doors that open of themselves? Objects and furniture moved by invisible hands? Or central heating, double glazing, the damp course, the renovation fanatic next door, small boys playing in forgotten or forbidden places, small creatures, oblivious of man and his worries, going about their daily lives? Or perhaps just time itself, tirelessly nibbling away day after day at a man-made, finite structure. Is what the witness experienced really paranormal? The investigator cannot assume that phenomena are paranormal simply because a witness thinks they are, or because at first sight they would appear to be, or because he himself would prefer that they were, but must try instead to unearth obvious natural causes which might at least have contributed to the experience. This is particularly important as the human mind (as noted in Chapter Twelve) tends to correlate unknown/unrecognizable with known/recognizable automatically.

Animals, birds and other creatures create noise in and around a house either because they are sufficiently large to cause it on their own account, or because they create changes in the fabric of the house which in turn cause those noises. Plumbing and other structural factors of a building make noise in and around the house either because they are reacting one upon the other, or are working inefficiently due to age or other causes. Small human beings have a sense of humour and moral ethics often unappreciated by larger members of the species, and are capable of producing a wide range of very peculiar noises and effects. The most mundane sounds can be translated by the imagination into footsteps, whispers, laughter and groans; and because the mind is capable of constructing from within itself those things which it feels ought to accompany known/recognizable sounds like footsteps, or whispers, and so on, a figure, too, may in some cases eventually appear. This will be completely subjective, and based upon a cause equally subjective, but it will nevertheless be there. Where a house is either old or remotely sited or very new indeed, and the phenomena experienced there appear to have 'snowballed', i.e. where footsteps or other apparently human sounds have preceded the sighting of an apparition, which has in turn preceded further and different effects, or where an apparition of a certain type has first been seen by only one member of a family, but eventually experienced by all, then an investigator should look most actively for a mundane first cause.

— *14* —

More Sites

Having completed a preliminary examination of witness and site, the investigator must go on to look for possible natural causes of the phenomena not visible to the naked eye, and also for historical facts and references which might go some way toward explaining and/or verifying the witness's experience. In order to do this, he will need a series of maps — town maps, ordnance survey maps, geological maps, in some cases maps which can only be examined at the borough surveyor's office — and access to various documents and records, as well as the use of his legs, his curiosity, and his common sense.

Maps come first — a paper version of the site proper and its surrounding environment. This stage of the investigation should begin with an examination of the relevant geological survey map.

Although geological survey maps are available in the western hemisphere for the whole world, they are expensive and not very easy to come by — usually, indeed, they have to be ordered — but, as they give complete details of the natural strata in the subsoil, and thus enable the investigator to see and evaluate what is going on underground, they are essential to proper investigation, and well worth the money.

Imagine, for example, that you are involved in an investigation at Cannock, in the county of Staffordshire, in the north of England. A geological survey map of Staffordshire will show that a very large proportion of the substructure of that county consists of coal. This fact is very important to the investigator, and might provide him with a vital clue in certain circumstances for, where coal exists, there are also mines.

Coal is no longer mined in Staffordshire as the pit faces are drowned, dangerous and unworkable, but the whole county was mined in the past, and very extensively, so that the entire area is now riddled with tunnels and shafts. The major effect of these tunnels is a tendency to subsidence, a fact of life with which the inhabitants of Staffordshire are very familiar indeed. It is not unknown for large and heavy vehicles to sink into the road on occasion, particularly during the winter months and when winters are very hard, but — of more interest to the investigator of psychical phenomena — it is subsidence, too, that causes buildings to crack, groan, and shift; walls and floors to fall out of true; traceries of cracks to appear in the tiled surfaces of kitchens and bathrooms practically overnight; windows and doors to open and close, and objects to move or fall to the ground, all apparently without human agency.

Such extensive underground tunnelling also causes sound to behave oddly. In some parts of Staffordshire sound carries for considerable and surprising distances, and it is distorted and mislocated over much of the area. Wind whistles through the old workings via a thousand points of entrance and egress large and small, with the effect, sometimes within buildings miles off from the real source of the sound, of conversations going on just below the level of hearing. Houses and workplaces, busy streets and empty county roads all echo with noises that might be distant gunfire, laughter, heavy footsteps, crowds of people shouting or running. Chambers and galleries far below the surface can, given the right conditions, cause one's own footsteps on the deserted road or pavement to create a subtle after-echo, giving the effect of a stealthy follower creeping along behind.

The production of such sound-effects as these is mitigated or enhanced by prevailing weather conditions, but the sounds themselves naturally always emanate from the same direction and always occur in the same place — it is this fact that will impress a witness, and not the fact that the phenomena are more pronounced when the wind is in a certain direction, or when frost lies thick on the ground, or when it is raining. It is, equally naturally, only too easy for the investigator to be so impressed as well, if he is not aware of the potential of a particular environment to produce such effects.

Staffordshire is a good example of an area in which 'mysterious' or allegedly paranormal phenomena are created on a daily basis by environmental conditions, but it is by no means the only place where this occurs. Neither, of course, are coal and mining the only subsoil factors which can create such effects. A sub-strata of chalk or clay can be equally productive of creaks, knocks, groans, and the movement of objects within buildings constructed on or near it, particularly when it rains heavily after a dry spell. Wetlands, sand and gravel too produce much the same effects in the same circumstances, because the buildings constructed on such substances settle (or even actually float, like Winchester cathedral, or the chapel of Marlborough College) on their foundations in wet weather conditions. So far as 'ghostly' figures are concerned, low lying, marshy, ground can produce startlingly human and lifelike mist figures at certain times of the day (most usually in the early morning and at twilight), and these can look amazingly real and purposeful as they drift and eddy in the wind — an illusion which is compounded where conditions are absolutely right, because the same figure will then appear at regular intervals in the same spot, and proceed to carry out much the same series of actions, thus mimicking a genuine haunting very well indeed.

Odd and apparently human sounds unaccompanied by any other real or apparent phenomena can be caused by tunnels of any kind, but sandstone conducts sounds even more efficiently — indeed, almost as efficiently as a telephone — and streams passing beneath buildings conduct sound in the same way, particularly when they are swollen. Lambert thought that it was a stream (swollen in 1885 by the River Chelt, which was in flood) passing under the Despard property that was the cause of the disturbances there, with the apparition having been added, as it were, by the imagination of Rosina Despard, and thereafter transmitted by her to the other witnesses, primarily because a noise at the door preceded the first appearance of the figure, and the phenomena practically ceased in 1886, the year when the Dowdeswell reservoirs were opened at the headwaters of the Chelt, thus reducing the water further downstream to a trickle. In my opinion, this theory does not adequately explain the events in the house, either while the Despards were living there or afterwards, but it at least serves to show the use of the geological survey map, and the care with which it needs to be studied, because, of course, Lambert's theory as to the haunting at Cheltenham cannot be ignored altogether.

Once the site has been examined and evaluated from the point of view of a geological survey map, the investigator must overlay that map with a more ordinary and readily accessible ordnance survey map which will show rivers, streams, roads, railway lines, large houses, airports and the like and relate the two into a sensible pattern.

A two-and-a-half-inch to the mile map will show surface features like wells, footpaths, houses, fields, forests and other natural features in greater detail, and a look at maps showing the man-made substructure of a town or village will only emphasize the possibility that mundane causes sometimes lie behind very astonishing phenomena. In the English town of Marlborough, for example, quite apart from the usual complement of sewers, water pipes, etc., nearly every building in the High Street is equipped with a spacious cellar (in fact it was once possible, I am told, to walk from one end of the High Street to the other through the adjoining cellars) and an astonishing number of them have wells under or behind them, most of which have never been filled in, and are in fact still full of good, albeit rather chalky, water. The sound effects there have to be heard to be believed.

All human habitation everywhere these days is riddled with pipes and passages, and where a site is very old rather than relatively new, then there will be more than might be expected. In some cases, too, pipes and sewers run parallel with streams, railway lines, busy roads, and the like, and this environmental accident will cause sound to be conducted very efficiently over quite a distance. The vibration of passing railway carriages is especially likely to carry in this way, particularly with underground trains, and the effect is not the rushing roar one might expect, but something quite different and infinitely more sinister, for sound rarely arrives at its destination 'whole', as it were, but undergoes considerable distortion on the way.

Thus it is that the investigator, having exhausted the potential of the visible parts of the site he is concerned with, must make himself aware of what is invisible before he rushes to the conclusion that he is dealing with, say, a real 'haunt' — and even when he has checked all that, he still can come to no concrete conclusion, for the early history and present usage of the site must be checked too.

The early history of any site is important even if the site itself is out of doors — in a forest say, or on farmland — because even if no building exists on the site now, one may once have stood there, and ghosts have in any event been known to continue to haunt a site despite structural alterations, demolitions and developments on or near it.

Imagine, for example, that the witness has reported seeing a woman, say, bending over something invisible in a field, a parking lot, or even in the middle of a motorway. Obviously, no house or human habitation exists on that spot now, but has this always been the case? Houses, indeed whole villages, have been known to disappear: our mythical woman may be bending over a well, long since filled in, that once provided water to a house or group of houses that have likewise gone to dust.

It is never wise, either, to assume that the usage of a building has remained unchanged, or that its name has not been changed even where the usage remains the same, or that what looks new (or old) actually is new (or old). The Chantry House at 99 High Street, Marlborough, for instance, once housed the priest of the Chantry of St Katherine, and contained an oratory, a dormitory, and a massive fifteenth-century` fireplace. The fireplace was removed in 1925 for export to America. The ground floor of the building has a modern frontage and is now occupied by Motor Aids. The upper storeys, replastered and sub-divided, are flats. The Chantry House is therefore to all intents and purposes unrecognizable for what it was, either inside or out, because so few of its original features remain actually visible to the naked eye. Lloyds Bank, on the other hand, at number 125, looks Elizabethan and might be accepted as such in a town where genuine Elizabethan properties abound — but it's a fake. Three gabled cottages did once stand there, but these were pulled down in 1885, and the building which replaced them was refaced — Elizabethanized — in 1930. The public house at number 46, however, has been a hostelry since 1626, but it has only been The Wellington Arms since 1845. Before that it was The King's Arms, and before that it existed for some years as The Golden Lion. Only old maps, documents and records — a surprising number of these exist — will show what, if anything, once stood on a site and, if anything did, what it was used for, when it was built and by whom.

Modern usage can be important, too, if only because quite ordinary sights can be misinterpreted so easily. If your witness reports seeing a cavalier, a roundhead, or an eighteenth-century gentleman, for example, striding out of the local community centre or public house, it is as well to check whether the amateur dramatics society was using the building on the night in question. It is as well to remember, too, that little local traditions could exist of which the witness might know nothing, and also that quite a lot of modern clothing is amazingly archaic in cut and design, while modern make-up can give an effect not altogether of this world in an ill-lit street on a dark night — particularly if met with unexpectedly at the close of a convivial evening.

Local museums and archaeological societies are the places to look for basic knowledge about the site and any early constructions there. If any did exist, the investigator should take careful note of what they were, what their function was, and when.

If, for example, the building previously extant on or near the site was a religious foundation of some kind, then it is possible that there are tunnels still in existence underground that might provide a perfectly acceptable and very mundane cause of any sounds heard, even though the building itself is gone. Of course, it is equally possible, too, that the haunt is real, because religious foundations (and closed communities in particular) breed such things. There is, after all, a concentration of thought generated in religious communities, and the existence of such a concentration is fundamental to at least one of the theories current as to the creation of ghosts.

There are rumours of tunnels like these in Marlborough, where the small remains of the priory that once flourished in the town now form part of an old people's home. However, Marlborough also has a ghostly monk, and tunnel and monk are happily conjoined, as the monk does not haunt the priory but another building which stands where the rumoured tunnel emerges. Whether the monk died in that building — or anywhere else in Marlborough — is quite immaterial. He probably lived in and formed part of the religious community there, and his consciousness was — and obviously still is — centred there.

Although no one need have died at the site for a haunting to result, the investigator must obviously try to find out whether anyone did, and if so, how, when and why. Violent deaths do not necessarily create ghosts, but the two are in many cases associated, so look for violent deaths first. Don't make the mistake of concentrating only on the victim where you do find record of a violent death. The murderer was a human being too, and was likely to have been in a considerable passion when the crime was committed. Remember, as well, that it is not enough to get vague information, and not useful at all just to establish that somebody (unnamed) died (of something unknown) in about, say, 1862 (or thereabouts). It is essential to find out *who* died and *how* and *when* and, further, to attempt to obtain documentary proof of it all. Miss Scott, you will recall, failed dismally at this, and that is why the story she found so believable is not really acceptable to us. Who was the clergyman at St Boswells? When did he die? If there really was a murder, who was killed, and when? The more information you can get, the better.

Again, and with religious sites in particular, it is obviously very necessary to find out what kind of religion was practised on the site and when, because, if it was Pagan, there could well have been sacrificial rites practised there that could adversely affect the atmosphere. However, not all Pagan religions practised human or any other kind of sacrifice, so make sure that the site in question belonged to, or was utilized by, a sect that did before you jump to conclusions — and try to find out as much as possible about ancient religious practices as they relate to the site in any event. There is a site on Jersey in the Channel Islands where a death associated with the religious practices of the day certainly occurred, and local people and visitors have had strange experiences there. However, the 'sacrifice' in this particular instance was a personal one: the victim starved himself to death.

Some Pagan sites are well documented, but most are not, and it wise to remember that some were co-opted by Christianity in ancient times. Where this latter is the case, the name given to the church built on the site is sometimes, but not always, indicative of its former use. Where it is not, then it is best to look within the environs of the present building for signs of why it might have been built there. Well worship and the like were deeply rooted in England, and so were proscribed by the early Church. If there is a well in the basement of the site, or perhaps some stone reputed to have healing properties, then that is probably the cause of the existence of the church on that spot.

Where no church or any other building, standing stone, or object having religious connotations exists on the site, but the witness's evidence and description seem to point to a religious context, then another look at maps might provide a timely clue. There are many archaeological and historical maps which give the location of settlements, roads, sacred sites, and the like — all of which can prove useful in establishing what, if anything, was where, and when.

It is always well worth while to research local folklore too, which often preserves, albeit in a distorted form, the beliefs and activities of former times. It is only comparatively recently, for example, that local people ceased to go to Silbury Hill in Wiltshire to make merry on Easter morning. How or why Silbury came to be associated with the Christian festival of Easter is not known, but one can certainly postulate that the original meaning of Silbury is at least remotely connected with the meaning of Easter in the Christian Church.

There is, of course, a great deal that is difficult about probing the past for information. Open ground upon which no habitation ever stood is a case in point, and the investigator's success or otherwise in those circumstances will often depend on the age of the haunt as it appears from the witness's description of what he has seen. If, for example, the witness reports the apparition as being dressed in modern clothing, or even clothing of apparently recent date, then the local police might be able to help. Local police forces are not unused to receiving reports of ghostly sitings, and are often quite helpful and not at all sceptical about them. Local newspapers too are useful even for events that took place up to 100 or more years ago, and local knowledge will often take the investigator further back than that, although this will necessarily be distorted. Where the haunt appears ancient, of course, none of these sources will help very much, save that they might reveal sightings earlier than that of your witness, but local historians, archaeologists and museums might be able to help pin-point era from costume, and event from era.

The local history of houses is often well-documented, and there is sometimes a record of who lived in them and when, but where constant rebuilding has gone on over the years on a single site, getting a complete record is practically impossible — and could be useless in the end, as one is never sure quite what one is looking for, even where the witness's description is detailed enough to provide adequate guidelines. It is still worthwhile, though, making 'overlays', i.e. plans of the various changes on the site, on sheets of clear plastic so that the general development of the building and its changing outline can be seen clearly. Overlays can often explain why the witness has reported activities on the part of the apparition incongruous with the present condition of the building — walking through walls, for instance, or appearing outside windows on the second storey. Where that is the case, the investigator's field of research is at least narrowed down to more manageable proportions. Where there is little documentation, however, or much confusing rebuilding, the name of the house, that of the street in which it stands, or the area of land around it, is sometimes indicative of original usage or owner and can be of help where all else fails.

To sum up: when the investigator is not looking for possible mundane causes of the witness's experience, then he is looking for confirmatory evidence to support it, and he is not likely to find either unless he works hard and conscientiously to that end. The recipe for a successful investigation is ample helpings of knowledge, curiosity, persistence, logic and hard graft, the whole lightly salted with imagination. It is *not* credulity and imagination, lightly seasoned with scraps of knowledge! So walk the ground. Get the maps and study them. Look up the meanings of local place-names. Investigate local folklore. If the site is in a village, talk to the older inhabitants of the place, for they are still the natural keepers of local history even in this day and age, and besides, they have the time and the desire to be interested in the minutiae of life in the area.

Visit the local highways department to find out if and when roads were altered, that is, raised, lowered, or moved altogether. Go to the rating authority to discover the age of the houses in the district, and who has lived in them and when. Search the church registers for the names of people who might fit the witness's description and who died during the period involved — sometimes the register will give the cause of death. Visit the local police station for a run-down on local gossip. Find out if the witness is alone in seeing his apparition, or whether someone else has seen it, and if so, when. Interview other witnesses if possible — and remember that, even where a witness has died, there may still be members of his family who heard his story from his own lips, or from someone else who did. Interview present residents to try to get the names of previous occupants. Go to the library for books on local history and to the newspaper offices for the popular and more detailed version of it. Above all, believe nothing that is not based in fact, and accept nothing at face value.

— *15* —

Coming to the Crunch

Once the information gained from maps, documents, records, people and places has been collated and the whole evaluated in the light of the witness's statement, the photographs, the scale plan and the investigator's own impressions of the site and witness, then he is in the best possible position to try to either reproduce the phenomena or experience them for himself. The way in which he now proceeds, the equipment he will need and the arrangements he must make, will, therefore, depend upon what it is he is trying to achieve, the site, the problem, and the depth of his pocket. Reproducing phenomena can be quite difficult sometimes, and frequently involves getting very dirty or contorting oneself into uncomfortable or unseemly positions, but it is usually a hurdle that can be got over with the use of a little imagination and common sense. Attempting to experience phenomena and record them mechanically, however, is quite another thing.

Let's look at equipment first. The type and amount of equipment required obviously depends on what exactly it is that the investigator is involved in, but, much of the time, necessary (as opposed to desirable!) equipment is fairly standard. Unfortunately, some items of standard equipment can be expensive, but it is not absolutely necessary that they should be, and the investigator can often get away with cheaper versions or alternatives. Sometimes, indeed, the simplest things work best. Absolute essentials are:

1. **A camera**. Ideally this should have time exposure controls, and a flash accessory. It should, if possible, also have a tripod. All of these things can be picked up second-hand, the only essentials being that the camera is reliable and that the operator knows how to work it!

There is no reason why the investigator shouldn't use a simple 'point click and wait for the picture' Polaroid — indeed, in some circumstances they are ideal.

Whether or not 'ghosts' can be photographed is a moot point, and the fact that there have been so many fraudulent 'spirit' photographs in the past has not helped matters at all, having rather created a prejudice against pictures of 'ghosts' instead. However, some few photographs do seem to be genuine (most of them taken by accident, as it were, by people bent on photographing chairs and staircases rather than 'ghosts') so it is worthwhile having a camera and using it. It might help to detect fraud, if nothing else.

2. **A supply of film** — high speed black-and-white and colour. A spare camera battery is also a good idea. An infra-red filter can be useful, so long as everyone knows if and when to use it. Film is quite expensive and developing even more so, but sadly there is no alternative to using quite a lot of it.

3. **A magnetic tape recorder**. This is not just to interview the witness, but also to attempt to record any sounds heard in a haunted building. These too can be picked up second-hand, and the same essentials apply to them as to cameras. There is no point in having (and lugging around) state-of-the-art sound equipment if someone can't make it work quickly and easily.

4. **A thermometer**. This should, if possible, be a large one, so that rapid rises or falls in temperature can be seen easily. Thermometers of this kind are obtainable from large chemists and garden centres, and they are quite cheap.

5. **Thin nylon thread, a reel of black cotton**, and **a packet of Blu-tack** (or similar adhesive material). These are not as cheap as they were, but still reasonable. They are used to detect physical agents moving objects, opening doors or travelling through rooms, thus either accidentally or deliberately causing fraudulent phenomena. Miss Despard used cotton and marine glue for the same purpose.

6. **A bag of flour, a bag of sugar, a packet of graphite powder** and **a small paintbrush**. Of these, only the graphite could be called dear. The graphite and the paintbrush are used to detect and highlight fingerprints, the flour is for detecting foot and hand prints, and the sugar is for scattering on the floor. It scrunches beautifully underfoot however lightly it is walked on, and so not only

provides physical evidence of intrusion, but also warns the investigator that the intruder is there.

7. **Chalk**. This is to circle ornaments and furniture so as to record any movement, and to mark walls if necessary.

8. **A spring balance and a strain gauge**. These record the weights of objects and the amount of force required to open doors, drawers and windows.

9. **A torch**, **candles** and **matches**. Only the torch might be expensive, because it is worthwhile getting a good one. Cheap ones are inclined to go out immediately if dropped, and thereafter decline to work at all. These items are all for working at night or in dark places.

10. **Notebooks** (plain paper and graph), **measuring tape**, **pens**, **pencils** and **crayons** for making rough plans and sketches, and keeping records. All are very reasonably priced.

11. **Adhesive tape**, **nylon twine**, **a ball of string**, **a stick of sealing wax**, **a packet of gummed labels** and **a packet of tie-on labels** — again, all quite cheap, and cheaper still if bought at a market rather than from a store. They are to seal rooms, passages, doorways and windows, so that no one may use them without the investigator's knowledge.

12. **A jar of honey**. A couple of pounds' worth will last a very long time indeed. Once spread on cotton, twine, etc., however thinly, honey will leave traces on whatever it subsequently touches for long periods of time because its stickiness does not 'dry'. It is very hard to remove without washing or dry-cleaning. This is for detecting the perpetrator of possible fraud.

13. **A Thermos flask** and/or **camping stove**, **kettle**, **mugs**, **a few sandwiches** and **some chocolate** — for vigils. The camping stove can be expensive, but not if bought from an army surplus store. If the investigator is on site for some hours, particularly if the site is uninhabited or situated out of doors, he will need sustenance to keep him warm and alert. It is hard to keep one's mind on the job in hand when very hungry or very cold.

14. **A good and reliable watch**, preferably with a luminous dial.

Naturally, special equipment can be constructed, and is very desirable in some circumstances. A camera can be attached to a thermostatic switch, for example, so that it will take a photograph immediately the temperature rises or falls. But unless expensive tracking devices are also attached, this still leaves the problem of where to point the camera before it can be left to get on with its job, and this is obviously best solved by the investigator staying with it and pointing it himself if at all possible.

This is another reason why working with a group of people is so much more desirable than working alone. One person cannot sit with a camera, look after and check other equipment, tour the site, record everything that is going on, and see everything there is to be seen. Neither is he likely to be adept at absolutely everything that needs to be done. Where a group is working together, tasks can be shared, and they can also be allotted to the person best qualified to complete them. Many hands make light work, and many minds preserve a balanced outlook. Useful people to have along are expert photographers and sound technicians, electricians, psychologists and clairvoyants. But proscribe anyone with a nervous disposition, however talented they may be. Investigation can be a strain on the nerves, and nervousness is contagious.

Where a group of people are working together, someone must first be elected to be in charge, and that decision must be adhered to for the length of the investigation. A schedule should thereafter be arranged and that should be adhered to as well, because there are many tasks that need to be completed in a timely and conscientious fashion, particularly if the site is indoors. For example:

1. At the commencement of each 'watch', the members of the group should synchronize their watches. The building should be searched thoroughly, all the doors and windows closed and fastened, and the garden or grounds (if any) inspected. This is a good time to ask for reactions from the clairvoyant if there is one present. A rota for further complete site checks should be formulated, and break and meal times for the separate members of the group agreed on. Observation posts should be set up, and each member of the group should know where they all are. A 'base' room should be decided upon, and meals and rest times taken there. All spare equipment should be kept in the 'base' room and everyone should know exactly where each item is.

2. If the phenomena are localized, then the affected part of the site must be sealed.

3. 'Watchers' should be placed at the various observation posts on the site.

4. Further tours of the building should take place at hourly intervals. Group members should take it in turn to do this, so that the general observation and work of the other members can go on unimpeded.

5. If any member of the group is capable of running a séance, then the group might want to meet at a specified hour to try this out — but don't do it if no one knows how.

6. If the building the investigator is working in is occupied, then the witness can be seconded as an assistant to one of the group — but he should not be allowed to work alone, for obvious reasons.

7. Again if the house is occupied, the investigator should be extremely careful about cleaning up when the 'watch' is over. Even if the building is empty or the site out of doors, no one should leave litter. It does matter.

Obviously, if the original phenomena took place out of doors, these guidelines must be amended to suit circumstances, and this is particularly the case where the witness was in a moving vehicle when the experience took place. Because of the distorting effect of light on the landscape, for instance, and its tendency to produce optical illusions, the investigator must be particularly careful about trying to reproduce as nearly as possible the experience of the witness as to time and positioning. The group should therefore arrive at the site at least an hour beforehand and, working from the original graph, so position its individual members as to be able to view the affected spot from a variety of angles, carefully noting the effect of the changing light.

If the witness's experience took place whilst he was driving a car or riding a bicycle, then obviously the whole group cannot usefully get into the vehicle, but at least one of them should complete the same journey, travelling at the same time and in the same way and preferably using the same mode of transport. The angle and breadth of vision afforded by a large car or truck are quite different to that afforded by, say, a Mini; and a person travelling on foot or on a bicycle has a very different psychological as well as physical outlook to a person travelling in a car — particularly on a dark and deserted country road. The other members of the group should position themselves around the affected spot and watch there, one standing as nearly as possible on the spot where the apparition appeared, so that the group member travelling in the car can carefully note the effect of a presence there on a person in a moving vehicle. In the same way, if the witness was walking when he had his experience, then one member of the group should walk, one should 'be' the apparition, and the others should distribute themselves about the affected spot.

In all cases, of course, people in charge of equipment should examine it regularly and carefully note down the results, and everyone should record their own movements and experiences, making sure to note the exact time these occur. *Don't leave this until later: do it as it happens.* Memories are fallible things.

If by chance an apparition does manifest and the particular member of the group who spots it is alone and out of sight of everyone else at the time, then he has the option of watching and following it, carefully noting down everything he can about it, or calling someone to come to him and risk disturbing the phenomenon so much that it dissipates. Probably the best thing to do is to strike a happy medium: watch first and attract somebody else's attention as subtly as possible where, when and if convenient. If two members of the group happen to experience phenomena together, they should not immediately turn one to the other and have an interesting chat about them. Write down impressions first: you can talk (and influence each other!) later.

Basically, once the investigator has arrived at this stage of the investigation, that is, assuming that he has failed to find a mundane reason for the witness's experience and so is trying not to reproduce it but to share it, then all he can do is get to the site, set up his equipment, work conscientiously, and do his best to cover all eventualities as they arise. As this will involve making a lot of notes, performing a lot of painstaking labour, completing a lot of routine checks and spending a lot of time waiting about, solitary, tobacco-less and alcohol-free, sometimes in darkness and usually in total silence, it is not often the unmitigated fun expected. Frequently the site is cold, wet, dirty, toiletless, spider-ridden or uncomfortable or all of the above. Sometimes the atmosphere is bad, and most of the time the whole exercise is unromantic and fruitless, productive only of a good crop of chilblains and a deep desire to see a bath and a bed. Unfortunately, there is little one can do about this. Investigations cannot be completed from an armchair and, so far as appointments with 'ghosts' are concerned, the investigator is free to choose neither place, nor time.

— *16* —

What If?

The investigator has weighed all the evidence in his own mind, separated primary from secondary effects, subjective from objective phenomena. He has labelled the case veridical or delusive, done everything he possibly can to shed light on the matter and he thinks he knows what he is looking at. If all has gone well, he will now be able to write his report, explain to the witness exactly what he is dealing with and why, and help him to come to terms with his experience. But what if things *haven't* gone well?

What if the investigator discovers that the phenomena have been created, deliberately or unconsciously, by the witness or one of his family or friends? What if he is sure in his own mind that the point of the exercise was a subconscious bid for attention, a cry for help, a deliberate attempt to drive someone out of lodgings or the family home, a smoke-screen to distract attention from a theft or series of thefts, a cloak for a love affair, or a ploy to obtain better housing or commercial advantage? What if the witness, intent on publicity, has given the investigator's name to the newspapers, and the gentlemen of the Press are standing on his doorstep? Or he finds an angry landlord on his hands, threatening proceedings? What if he needs a medium or a clergyman? Or advice on how to proceed from some experienced person, either as to equipment or some other thing? What if, having commenced the investigation, and taken it as far as he can, he decides he can't handle it and needs help?

Let's take deliberate fraud first. Unfortunately there is really very little anyone can do about it. Sometimes the arrival of an investigator, fully equipped and asking awkward questions, is enough to strangle the idea of deliberate fraud at birth, and the case will die a natural death after the first interview. Quite a lot of people with fraud in mind have picked up enough about psychic phenomena to be able to reproduce them or at least describe them adequately but, knowing little or nothing about investigators, are unpleasantly surprised by the arrival of a person not nearly so gullible as they had hoped. If matters do continue past the first interview, then sometimes a subtle hint to the suspected perpetrator(s) will do the trick and the phenomena will peter out and finally cease altogether. But the subtle hint is the last weapon in the investigator's armoury. If it is not enough, then he can only withdraw politely and decline further involvement. There is no point in making public (or even private) accusations, and he should not do so. Where a fraud is being perpetrated because the witness is living in unsuitable housing or conditions, or because he has serious financial or social problems, then the investigator may find that he has considerable sympathy with him, but he should not get involved, nor even offer advice. He is not a social worker or a financial advisor, and can do neither the witness nor himself any good by pretending that he is.

Much the same comments apply where the witness or a member of his household is the victim of malice or a hoax. The investigator can't intervene between the protagonists or even show sympathy to one and displeasure to the other, for he can do no good and might make matters worse. Again, he can drop a hint to the perpetrator(s) or, if the perpetrators are young children, to their parents, and hope that a nod will be as good as a wink, but that is all. He can't make accusations, or be drawn into explanation or argument — this is quite pointless and can result in considerable and open ill-feeling.

If he thinks that the witness or one of his family, household, or friends has unconsciously created the phenomena, then he *is*, alas, going to have to say so, explaining his reasoning as cogently as he can to the head of the house, or to those persons he feels will respond most sympathetically. This denouement is unlikely to be greeted with cries of delight, but at least it need not take place in the presence of the person responsible for the problem — indeed, it should not do so, as recriminations are likely to instantly result if it does, and this will not help matters at all. The points to stress are that the problem will cease if the underlying cause is dealt with or removed, and that direct accusation or exposure will not assist to that end. Again, the investigator should neither show sympathy nor offer advice to either the perpetrator or the victims, whatever his own feelings may be. Obviously, he should be very sure of his facts before he mentions the matter at all.

If the witness has given his name to the Press, the investigator's best course of action is to refuse to comment at all in the first instance. He should not be drawn into conversation with reporters until he has worked out to his own satisfaction just how the land lies and what his witness's motive was in approaching the media in the first place. Newspaper representatives have a way of editing conversation to suit themselves, usually with unhappy results. No one, of course, can stop the witness talking to the Press, but the investigator can refuse to have anything to do with them himself if he thinks such a course would be unwise. Where the Press have been tipped off by someone other than the witness, then he should impress upon the latter the wisdom of his saying nothing to them either. A newspaper will rarely print anything that is not confirmed by someone directly involved.

If the witness has reported the matter to the Press in detail, and this has resulted in the investigator being approached by third parties, such as the landlord or owner of any affected property, then he should consult a solicitor immediately, and refer all callers to him. He should not make statements to anyone except his solicitor. Having hired a dog, he can rest content to let it get on and do all the necessary barking.

If a medium is needed, then remember that the word 'medium' needs to be qualified by the words 'reputable' and 'experienced'. The investigator should remember, too, that if he is not used to working with mediums, he cannot just obtain the services of such a person and then expect him or her to take charge and perform miracles. Mediums and mediumship need to be handled with care if damage is not to result, so if the investigator has never worked with a medium at all, his first requirement is really a medium *and* at least one person who is used to working with same. For investigators in Britain, the College of Psychic Studies at 16 Queensberry Place, London SW7 2EB is a good and reputable organization which may be able to help with suggestions and/or introductions to mediums who might be willing and able to work with investigations.

It should be borne in mind, though, before taking such a step, that however experienced and reputable the medium, everything he says cannot be taken as gospel, and also that it must be ensured that the controls exercised over him are as stringent as those constructed for the witness and the investigator. The evidence produced by way of mediumship is always interesting and often helpful to the investigator, but it can rarely be proved authentic, and the scientific establishment is unlikely to accept the results of an investigation that is based directly upon it. As confirmatory evidence, however, it can be very useful, and if the controls have been good enough no one is likely is reject it out of hand. Genuine mediums will never object to such controls being set.

If a clergyman is needed, particularly with a view to performing an exorcism, then, in England at least, it will be necessary to approach a bishop of the Church of England or of Rome. Exorcists are still appointed by both Churches, although neither body will produce one at the drop of a hat. The Church of England published a report on the subject of exorcism in 1972 which recommended, among other things, that medical advice be sought to avoid the possibility of anyone suffering by virtue of the ritual, that no exorcism be carried out without the permission of a bishop, and that a Diocesan Exorcist be appointed wherever the need arose. Not all Church of England bishops appoint such an expert as a matter of course, and getting an exorcist, whether from the Church of England or the Roman Catholic Church, is unlikely to be a speedy affair, both bodies very rightly viewing the matter as something not to be undertaken lightly.

The need for exorcism in cases of haunting is in any case moot, but if the witness and his household feel that they would be the better for it, then it will be for the investigator to assist them to try to make arrangements for an exorcism to be carried out. Obviously, the investigator's notes, records and observations will be of assistance to the person into whose hands the matter finally falls, and he should make the relevant copies and hold himself in readiness for any interview accordingly.

If advice is needed as to equipment or as to how to proceed, or the investigator feels that the matter is beyond him and that he cannot continue with it unaided, then in Britain he should approach the Society for Psychical Research at 1, Adam & Eve Mews, London W8 6UQ, where there exists a friendly staff and an excellent library. Advice is free, the use of the library is free to members, and membership is both reasonable and very useful.

Good luck with your 'ghosts'.

Emily Peach
Marlborough, February 1990

Select Bibliography

Abdy-Collins, B., *The Cheltenham Ghost*, Psychic Press Limited, 1948.

Ashby, R.H., *Guide Book for the Study of Psychical Research*, Rider Press, 1972.

Beard, Paul, *Survival of Death*, Pilgrim Books, 1983.

— *Living On*, Pilgrim Books, 1987.

Bennett, Ernest, *Apparitions and Haunted Houses*, Faber & Faber, 1939.

Broad, C.D., *Lectures on Psychical Research*, Routledge & Kegan Paul, 1962.

— 'Phantasms of the Living and of the Dead' in *Proceedings of the SPR*, Vol.50, Pt.183, 1953, pp.51–66.

Butler, W.E., *Telepathy & Clairvoyance*, Warner Destiny, 1978.

Finucane, R.C., *Appearances of the Dead: A Cultural History of Ghosts*, Junction Books, 1982.

Fortune, D., *Through The Gates of Death*, Samuel Weiser Inc., 1979.

Garrett, Eileen, *Adventures in the Supernormal*, Garrett Publications, 1949.

Gauld, Alan, *Mediumship and Survival*, Paladin Press, 1983.

Green, Celia and McCreery, C., *Apparitions*, Hamish Hamilton, 1976.

Gurney E., Myers F.W.H. and Podmore F., *Phantasms of the Living*, Trubner & Co., 1886.

Haining, Peter, *Ghosts: The Illustrated History*, Sidgwick & Jackson, 1974.

Hart, Professor H. and Associates, 'Six Theories About Apparitions' in *Proceedings of the SPR*, Vol.50, Pt.185, 1956, pp.153–239.

Hudson, Thomson Jay, *The Law of Psychic Phenomena*, G.P. Putnams Sons Limited, 1920.

Johnson, Raynor, *Psychical Research*, English University Press, 1955.

Lambert, G.W., 'The Use of Evidence in Psychical Research' in *Proceedings of the SPR*, Vol.50, Pt.185, 1956, pp.275–93.

Mackenzie, A., *Hauntings and Apparitions*, Paladin Press, 1983.

Muldoon, S.J. and Carrington, H., *The Phenomena of Astral Projection*, Rider Press, 1951.

Myers, F.W.H., *Human Personality and its Survival of Bodily Death*, Longman, 1903.

Pearce-Higgins, J.D. and Whitby, G.S., *Life, Death and Psychical Research*, Rider Press, 1973.

Salter, W.H., *Ghosts and Apparitions*, G.Bell & Sons Limited, 1938.

— *Trance Mediumship*, Society for Psychical Research, 1950.

Salter, Mrs W.H., *Evidence For Telepathy*, Sidgwick & Jackson, 1934.

Sidgwick, Mrs H., 'Notes on the Evidence, Collected by the Society, for Phantasms of the Dead' in *Proceedings of the SPR*, Vol.3, 1885, pp.69–150.

Stevens, W.O., *Unbidden Guests*.

Tyrrell, G.N.M., *Apparitions*, The Society for Psychical Research, 1973.

West, D.J., 'The Investigation of Spontaneous Cases' in *Proceedings of the SPR*, Vol.48, 1948, pp.264–300.

Index

NUNC SAPIENTIS OSSA MERLINI UBI

Discover Tarot

Understanding and Using Tarot Symbolism

Emily Peach

Discover Tarot is a radical new approach to understanding and using Tarot. Originally published as the best-selling *Tarot Workbook*, it contains a carefully graded course of practical exercises designed to give the student a sound working knowledge of Tarot symbolism and interpretation in the shortest possible time.

Emily Peach shows how Tarot cards can be used both as accurate divinatory tools and as powerful means of deepening psychological and spiritual awareness. The result is a comprehensive, 'user-friendly' manual that provides an easy-to-follow guide to assimilating and applying the symbolic wisdom of the Tarot. Amongst the many topics covered are:

- getting to know the Tarot
- understanding the symbolism of the Major and Minor Arcanas
- fortune-telling by Tarot
- how to give readings and types of spreads
- meditation and visualization techniques
- the Tarot and the Tree of Life

The Poltergeist Experience

Investigations into Ghostly Phenomena

D. Scott Rogo

Explosions of crockery . . . mysterious outbreaks of fire . . .
strange nocturnal noises . . . eerie levitations — poltergeist
phenomena like these are among the most baffling and terri-
fying experiences known to man. Now D. Scott Rogo re-
evaluates everything science and philosophy have learned
about poltergeists and demonstrates how, far from being mal-
evolent spirits of the dead, they appear to be the result of deep
psychological conflicts, repressed hatreds, buried frustrations
— psychokinetic projections from the subconscious mind.

Bringing the history of the poltergeist right up to date, *The
Poltergeist Experience* focuses on how modern psychology has
given researchers the tools to investigate and study the people
and situations behind disturbances. Furthermore, it offers a
bold new theory to explain the intelligence and face behind
the poltergeist and — liberally spiced with accounts of the
author's own remarkable experiences — is the first book of its
kind to show how to *cure* poltergeist sufferers.

Combatting Cult Mind Control

Protection, Rescue and Recovery from
Destructive Cults

Steven Hassan

Today experts agree that destructive cults are burgeoning and infiltrating new areas of society, including big business, the legal system and government.

Combatting Cult Mind Control presents the startling facts about destructive cults, focusing on their use of psychological manipulation to gain money, power and influence. Steven Hassan, a defector from the upper echelon of a controversial cult, gives an inside view on the methods used to recruit and control members, the psychology behind these techniques and practical means of identifying them. His compelling portrayal of cult life, which includes the chilling story of his own recruitment and indoctrination, shows how mind control techniques can inflict serious psychological damage and leave an individual unable to think for himself.

Now working as a counsellor, helping people to break away from cults and return to society, Hassan presents a unique strategy for recovery, re-education and rescuing a loved one from a destructive cult without coercion, stressing the importance of approaching cult members with compassion rather than condemnation. Specific guidance is given for distinguishing destructive cults from legitimate organizations and protecting ourselves, friends and families from the tyranny of cult mind control.

'Well worth reading, because early recognition and appropriate intervention depend on greater awareness of this menace:
—Peter Tyrer, *The Lancet*

'MUST reading for anyone who has been touched by the cult phenomena, their friends and loved ones, and all those concerned with preserving freedom in our society.'
—Carol Giambalvo, FOCUS